47/6

ORCHID GROWING
FOR EVERYONE

ORCHID GROWING FOR EVERYONE

Tropical and Sub-Tropical

by

KARL MATHO

(Late of the Botanical Gardens, Hamburg)

With 64 full colour plates by
ANNE GALLION-KROHN

BLANDFORD PRESS
LONDON

First published in English in 1958
© *Copyright Blandford Press Ltd.*
16 West Central Street, London W.C.I.

Printed in Holland
by The Ysel Press, Deventer

CONTENTS

Plates in colour 7

Foreword 9

PART I   Introduction 11

Chapter 1   Geographical Distribution 15

Chapter 2   Habits of the Orchid 19
           Orchids growing in soil (Terrestrial) 20
           Orchids growing in humus (Saprophytic) .. 21
           Orchids growing on trees (Epiphytic) 22

Chapter 3   Biology and Morphology of the plant organs .. 27
           Roots.................................. 27
           Pseudo-bulbs: stems 28
           Leaves 29
           Inflorescence 30
           Flowers 31

Chapter 4   Structure of the Orchid flower 33
           Diandrous 35
           Monandrous 37

Chapter 5   Propagation of Orchids 46
           Sexual reproduction 46
           Symbiotic sowing 46
           Asymbiotic sowing 47
           Sowing on culture medium 48
           Pricking off and transplanting 48
           Further cultivation 49
           Vegetative propagation 51
           Cuttings 51
           Division 52
           Mycorrhiza 53

Chapter 6   Orchids as Indoor Plants 55
           Light conditions 56

Watering............................. 57
Concentration of Hydrogen ions 58
Correct watering 60
Humidity 61
Fresh air 62
Temperatures 63
Composts and their preparation 64
Mixing of composts 65
Growing in pots 68
Repotting 68
Manuring 72
Pests and how to combat them 75

Systematic classification (according to Pfitzer) 78
Notes on the classificatlon 81

PART II   Special Section with coloured plates 97
A selection of indoor orchids 163
Abbreviations of names of authorities 165
Index................................. 167

PLATES IN COLOUR

		Page
1	Paphiopedilum bellatum	97
2	Paphiopedilum curtisii	98
3	Paphiopedilum insigne var, sanderae	99
4	Paphiopedilum rothschildianum	100
5	Paphiopedilum sanderianum	101
6	Paphiopedilum venustum	102
7	Disa uniflora	103
8	Epidendrum schomburgkii	104
8	Epidendrum radicans	104
9	Epidendrum cooperianum	105
10	Epidendrum raniferum	106
11	Masdevallia backhousiana	107
12	Masdevallia shuttleworthii	108
13	Coelogyne cristata	109
14	Coelogyne speciosa	110
15	Barkeria spectabilis	111
16	Cattleya bowringiana	112
17	Cattleya citrina	113
18	Cattleya dowiana	114
19	Cattleya warscewiczii	115
20	Dendrobium chrysotoxum	116
21	Dendrobium nobile	117
22	Dendrobium phalaenopsis	118
23	Dendrobium pierardi	119
24	Laelia cinnabarina	120
24	Laelia flava	120
25	Laelia purpurata	121
26	Laelia tenebrosa	122
27	Brassavola nodosa	123
28	Ansellia africana	124
29	Calanthe vestita	125
30	Chysis bractescens	126
31	Phajus tankervilliae	127
32	Cirrhopetalum makoyanum	128
33	Cyrtopodium andersonii	129
34	Eulophia guineensis	130
35	Cymbidium lowianum	131
36	Catasetum macrocarpum	132
37	Catasetum tabulare	133
38	Cycnoches chlorochilum	134
39	Stanhopea graveolens	135
40	Sophronitis coccinea	136
40	Sophronitis cernua	136

Page

41 Anguloa brevilabris.............................. 137
42 Lycaste aromatica................................ 138
43 Lycaste skinneri 139
44 Zygopetalum mackayi 140
45 Maxillaria picta 141
46 Maxillaria sanderiana 142
47 Trichopilia tortilis 143
48 Miltonia spectabilis 144
49 Miltonia vexillaria 145
50 Odontoglossum crispum 146
51 Odontoglossum grande 147
52 Odontoglossum insleayi 148
53 Odontoglossum rossii 149
54 Oncidium jonesianum 150
55 Oncidium lanceanum 151
56 Oncidium papilio 152
57 Oncidium splendidum............................ 153
57 Oncidium varicosum var. rogersii.................. 153
58 Angraecum sesquipedale 154
59 Euanthe sanderiana 155
60 Phalaenopsis aphrodite 156
61 Phalaenopsis luddemanniana 157
62 Phalaenopsis stuartiana 158
63 Vanda coerulea 159
64 Vanda teres 160

LIST OF DIAGRAMS

Fig.
1   A Diagram of a Liliaceae   33
    B Diagram of a Diandrous Orchid ....
    C Diagram of a Monandrous Orchid ....
2   Diandrous Flower   35
3   Monandrous Flower   38

FOREWORD

This book is the fruit of many years' intensive study of these lovely and mysterious flowers. Its aim is to open up a sphere of rare wonders to a wide circle of nature lovers, particularly lovers of fine flowers, and thereby inspire new enthusiasts. May it awaken in many the desire to own and cultivate orchids for themselves. With a little understanding and a wise choice, satisfactory results can soon be obtained.

The material is almost inexhaustible and in a book only a modest selection is possible, but it will probably be sufficient to give a fair idea of the tremendous range of this family of plants.

A word or two about the coloured plates, which are the work of the well-known artist, Anne Gallion-Krohn. I should like here to express my thanks to her and my appreciation of her delicate skill. Most of her pictures have been drawn from life. I should also like to thank Dr. E. Bohnert, President of the German Orchid Society in Hamburg, Georg Vorwerk and Heinrich Wilhelm, also of Hamburg, and all the workers in the botanical gardens for their varied and friendly assistance.

Hamburg   Karl Matho.

INTRODUCTION

Nature is full of wonders. One of the most glorious she has produced, and certainly one of the most exciting, is the orchid, for here flower formation has reached perfection. Anyone who has stood in rapt contemplation before such a magic picture will understand with what wonder and excitement collectors in the Old World beheld their first orchids—those ambassadors, as it were, from the depths of the tropics. But they were shrouded in mysteries whose revelation proved of absorbing interest to generations of scholars.

It is easy to understand why an immediate desire to possess orchids arose from this admiration and enthusiasm for them. For a good while their possession was, of course, possible only by the wealthy. These plants, very rare at first and easily destroyed, could not be cheap; they grew in far off countries in the most inaccessible spots. Anyone who wished to find them had to brave the dangers of the tropical forest and the climate without thought for his own life. It was often a matter of using the most primitive methods for felling gigantic trees in whose tops the precious blooms made their habitat, and there gradually grew up an occupation surrounded with a halo of adventure—the profession of orchid hunting. It has survived to the present day.

Added to these dangers were the difficulties of transport, mostly carried out in canoes on rivers with swift-flowing rapids. Whole cargoes were often lost through the canoes capsizing and it was not uncommon for the hunter to lose his life as well. Even when the coast was successfully reached, fresh dangers threatened on the long sea journey. For many years a large number of consignments fell victim to these risks, until sufficient experience in handling and packing them had been accumulated.

Undertakings of this kind involving great cost and a high rate of loss compelled the buyers to put their prices up; for a good new discovery they often asked and received £1,000 and in some cases much more. About 1800 the first buyers in the market were British horticultural firms. They procured orchids solely for the old nobility, who soon became very attached to these mysterious flowers. For a long time it was never possible fully to meet the demand from the first meagre consignments and so orchid-growing was confined in these early days to Britain. Only after saturation point had been reached in England and prices for orchid plants had fallen a good deal did people begin, first in France then later on in Germany, to start cultivating them.

In England the value of breeding new types with better flowering possibilities was very soon recognised. The English raised the hybridisation of the *Odontoglossum* and *Paphiopedilum* species to a particularly high level, but they were also very successful with other kinds and today England is known as the 'classic' land of the orchid.

Soon other new hybrids appeared, and only when growers had learnt the systematic cultivation of orchids, about the turn of the century, did prices come more within the reach of a greater number of people. Today they have arrived at the point where they are hardly dearer than other indoor plants apart, of course, from the very special kinds and expensive varieties. There are now plenty of varieties which under appropriate conditions, it is quite possible to grow indoors.

Although in the course of time the cultivation of orchids reached a high standard, growing young plants from seed remained uncertain and problematical. Successful sowings alternated with greater failures and growers were perplexed until the French botanist, Noel Bernard, succeeded in solving the problem in 1904, almost 200 years after the discovery of the first of these exotic plants.

He was able to show how orchids in the natural state germinate only with the help of a fungus that lives in the roots of the mother plant (symbiosis), for the tiny little seed of the orchid comes off badly in life before germination, as compared with that of the large bean or pea. Whilst the embryo in a bean seed, already well-developed, is abundantly supplied with nourishment, the orchid seed has only a few feeding cells. With these alone it is not capable of starting its new life. Although this was a striking new discovery, it was not known how to make immediate

practical use of it. The questions which arose were so revolution-
ary and novel that they could only be answered by laborious
detailed work and complicated scientific experiments in labora-
tories.

Bernard's discovery showed that orchid seeds, as they were
then being sown by the gardeners, had now to be inoculated
with the root fungus of the mother plant, if they were to be
successfully reared. It is also to Bernard's credit that he developed this method of sowing, which follows nature so closely, and is
called 'symbiotic'. The well known German orchid expert,
Professor Burgeff, extended and enriched this knowledge considerably. His popular book *Germinating of Orchid Seeds* was the
first one to give deeper insight into the secrets of germination and
the directions necessary for their practical use. This required
the extraction of the appropriate fungus from the root cells of
the mother plant. It had to be kept a pure culture by an appropriate process i.e. keeping it free from parasitic fungi and
bacteria—a task that it was virtually impossible to carry out.

After long experiments, an American scientist, Knudson,
succeeded in developing, a method of growing without a fungus,
which made the work considerably easier. It is known as asymbiotic culture, in which the root fungus is replaced by a sugar
solution. It has already proved its worth in practice. The
procedure for both methods, the symbiotic (with fungus) and
the asymbiotic (without fungus), will be gone into later on when
we come to the propagation of orchids. They demand not only
specialised knowledge but also a mastery of scientific methods
which in their turn are only possible with expensive apparatus.

If the symbiotic method had already brought about a considerable increase in the growing of young plants, it was now to be
improved by the asymbiotic method, which nearly all the
specialised nurseries adopted. The way was open for a systematic
and more certain cultivation on a broader basis. Growers got a
new impetus and produced countless new varieties. Most of those
on sale today are, therefore, not original kinds as found in
nature, but hybrids.

The effect of this successful growing was not only that prices fell, but that imports were no longer needed. And it was high time for through mass-exploitation of reserves many species had nearly died out, and the governments of the various overseas countries were compelled to promulgate laws for the protection and maintenance of their orchids.

CHAPTER I

GEOGRAPHICAL DISTRIBUTION

If we want to go more deeply into the wonderful world of the orchid and see that each kind has its proper care, we must know something about its natural living conditions, origin and native surroundings. It is of course not possible within the compass of this book to give exhaustive information even about the main species. As early as 1927 Schlechter pointed out, in his book on orchids, that 15,000 kinds had already been described. Since then some 100 new discoveries have been made every year, so that with close on 20,000 varieties the orchids now form the largest plant family in the world.

From such a selection it was a matter of making a choice of the finest, best known and most widely cultivated varieties. Further information about their habitat is to be found either in the table on page 163 or in the descriptions of the individual plants. In general it may also be said that orchids comprise not only the most numerous but the most widespread family as well. They grow in all the five continents and almost every region.

It is an interesting fact that the orchids which grow on trees only occur in the tropics and, less frequently, the sub-tropics, that is in the belt which extends for about 12 degrees on both sides of the equator. According to Schlechter this area contains 85% of all varieties. The tree-loving species are found here in their perfect element. Abundant rainfall is spread throughout the whole year and there is no change of season such as is usual in our part of the world. The warm humid atmosphere essential to these orchids is produced by the high temperature under a thick covering of foliage. Living as they do anything up to 150 feet from the ground they are unable to get water from the soil as do those growing on the ground. The further you move away from the tropics the less numerous this type becomes and the kinds that grow on trees tend more and more to be displaced by those that grow in soil until eventually, in the temperate zones, only the latter are to be found. Here of course they adapt themselves to a wholly different climate. The parts above ground die off in winter like perennials, and new shoots are formed in the spring. Even in the sub-tropics, which have an alternation of wet and dry seasons in place of our winter and summer, many terrestrial varieties have the same periodic growth.

On the whole each of the five continents has its own characteristic types of orchid. If there is an overlapping of types from one continent to another this never occurs with the same species but only with the different ones within the same genus.

A few orchids of the temperate zones are an exception to this rule. They appear in other parts of the world wherever they find their own peculiar living conditions.

Africa and Australia are very poor in the more valuable orchids. Of well-known species the latter has only *Dendrobiums* and *Cymbidiums* to show. One might mention *Angraecum* and *Ansellia* from Africa and the very beautiful terrestrial *Disa* which are unfortunately gradually dying out owing to over-exploitation. They grow in the temperate region of South Africa and strict laws have been made by the Union to protect them. That is why we hardly ever come across them here in Europe.

On the island of Madagascar off the South-west coast of Africa is found, amongst others, the *Angraecum sesquipedale* (Thouars du Petit) (Plate 58) which is known everywhere on account of its imposing shape. It is endemic, that is to say it is only to be found in the island. If recent reports are true that the ancient forests in which it grows are to be burnt down this magnificent variety will, unfortunately, become extinct.

Endemic *Cymbidiums* are also found on Madagascar, indeed the island is famous for its endemic species. Such plants, occupying only certain areas or districts within their continent, are met with in nearly every part of the world.

If Africa and Australia have, as has already been said, little to show in the way of the finest orchids, in the other tropical zones

we find an abundant variety, from the Himalayas in East Asia
to the American continent, taking in tropical India and the
extensive Malayan archipelago, but it is principally the tropics
of Central and South America that offer an incomparable wealth
of the most unusual and beautiful orchids.

The slopes of the Himalayas are the home of many well-known
genera: *Dendrobium,* found up to more than 6,000 feet, varieties
of *Coelogyne* and *Vanda,* among them the exquisite *Vanda
coerulea* which is still found in Burma, and varieties of *Cymbidium*
which grow in soil.

In East Asia we find varieties of Pfitzer's *Paphiopedilum
insigne* (Plate 3) widely known as lady's slipper and often wrongly
called *Cypripedium.* Its numerous relatives are found in the
Malayan Archipelago and represent a particularly charming
type with variegated foliage. On account of their richness of form
they have become very popular as table-flowers.

The better-known terrestrial genera *Calanthe, Cyrtopodium*
and *Phajus* come from the tropical regions of India. Besides
quantities of less glamorous orchids you find here and in the
Malayan islands species of *Dendrobium, Coelogyne, Cymbidium,
Bulbophyllum, Cirrhopetalum* and *Vanda.* The islands of Borneo
and the Philippines are known for different species of the
wonderful moth-orchid, *Phalaenopsis,* and of the *Dendrochilum,*
with their delicate and charming blooms.

The orchids of tropical America are abundant in number but
scattered; only a few species from the Old World spill over into
this continent. The genera here are nearly all new ones, as many
as a hundred different kinds. Only the most important can be
mentioned here. Their representatives have long since won a
sure place in our hearts on account of their beauty.

The most famous is the genus *Cattleya* with its large sweet-
smelling blooms. Their different types extend to the tropical
forests of Brazil, Colombia, Mexico, Venezuela and Peru. Bate-
man's exquisite yellow *Cattleya dowiana,* however, is to be found
in Costa Rica. Reichenbach junior's *Cattelya percivaliana* grows
on rocks in Venezuela, and can be found up to 4,000 feet. It does
not grow on trees. In the upper levels of the equatorial Andes are

to be found the *Odontoglossum* and *Masdevallia*. On account of the height at which they grow, 5,500-6800 feet, they are cultivated as coolhouse plants here.

Mention must be made of further noteworthy genera which grow in this tropical belt, such as *Laelia*, which closely resembles *Cattleya*, *Acineta*, *Anguloa*, *Bifrenaria*, *Brassavola*, *Brassia*, *Catasetum*, *Cycnoches*, *Epidendrum*, *Gongora*, *Lycaste*, *Maxillaria*, *Miltonia*, *Oncidium* with their large variety of shapes, *Schomburgkia*, whose hollow bulbs shelter ants, *Stanhopea*, with their unusual hanging blooms, and *Zygopetalum*.

This by no means exhausts their number. The so-called botanical genera which are rather more modest in appearance are present in vast quantities.

CHAPTER II

HABITS OF THE ORCHID

As far as living conditions are concerned, all plants are bound by natural laws, particularly changes of season. Orchids, highly skilled in adaptation, are no exception. They prosper under the most diverse environments and get from them their characteristic size and shape. These conditions are chiefly determined by climate, soil and position, which vary considerably from region to region and continent to continent.

We have already seen how far peculiarities can extend with orchids. It is the same with their habits which are conditioned by their locality. These very conditions demand our careful attention because they give valuable clues as to how to grow them.

Orchids are not only found in grassland, in hilly country and meadows high up in the mountains of the temperate zones, but also on the savannahs and less densely-wooded areas of the sub-tropics and to a lesser extent in the shady edges and clearings of the misty and rain-soaked forests of the tropics. These grow in soil and are known as Terrestrial Orchids. Another and very remarkable group has selected the humus found in the shade or half shade of woods in every zone. These are called humus plants and are known as Saprophytes. But the largest, and for us most interesting, group is formed by those orchids which have chosen tropical or sub-tropical trees to live in and so are called Epiphytes (tree dwellers). Sometimes epiphytic types become terrestrial, e.g., the *Catasetum* species and some representatives of a few other genera for they can also be found growing on rocks. Others grow at astonishing heights almost up to the snow-line of tropical mountain ranges. Stein's *Book of the Orchid* gives heights up to 10,000 feet above sea-level for many types of the

Odontoglossum genus, whose Eldorado lies particularly in the Andes and the Cordilleras of Central and South America. Although these mountain ranges lie within the equatorial zone, at such heights sub-alpine climates obtain, only the snow-line is forced higher, to about 12,000 feet. It is extremely important to know this when growing orchids that come from these parts. It must also be taken into consideration that they are accustomed to mist, dew and excessive rain. But although every zone and every region has its own climatic conditions, these plants are not so dependent on natural conditions of growth as would appear at first sight.

Orchids then can be divided into three main groups according to their habit, each with its own peculiarities:

(1) Terrestrial.
(2) Saprophytic.
(3) Epiphytic.

TERRESTRIAL ORCHIDS OR ORCHIDS GROWING IN SOIL

The terrestrial orchids of the temperate zones are mostly small, unpretentious plants whose organs are suited to the interchange of summer and winter. They possess various kinds of tuber which store up reserves of food like our native orchids, some of which are medicinal, They produce a tuber or they have a tap-root that throws out shoots.

A few beautiful North American kinds, such as the *C. reginae* grow readily in Europe and make a splendid show in the garden. *Bletilla striata* (Bletia) from China and Japan also grow in any garden soil and are very showy. But they must all be well covered with leaves in order to protect them from the severe winter weather.

Most of the terrestrial orchids remain under ground during the winter. The parts above ground die off and the plant is reduced to its bulbs and their roots.

Orchids growing in temperate zones do the same. The climate imposes a dry season on them which is comparable to our winter. Though many species in this climate remain evergreen, others lose their stems and leaves, while yet others have strong pseudo-bulbs which throw off their leaves only in the dry season so as to minimise evaporation.

On the other hand, in the tropics the relatively small number of terrestrial orchids are evergreen because of the more settled climate.

SAPROPHYTIC ORCHIDS (growing in humus)
(Greek sapros = rotting : phyton = plant)

This relatively small group is of no use for garden purposes, but botanically it is both curious and highly interesting. The plants grow on the ground in forests of every zone. They are described as Saprophytic because they can live only in the rotting humus which is provided by the leaf mould of fir and other trees. Their peculiarity lies in the extravagant nature of their nourishment which their structure and habits reflect in the most striking way. The plants are mostly pale in colour and are able to live without assimilating carbon. The flowering stalk is almost without a joint. It may be white, yellow, brown or violet in colour. Astonishingly enough there are no leaves; they are reduced to a sheath or scale. As the plants do not need any chlorophyll they can do without leaves and in most cases the flowers are the same colour as the stem. Now and again they may be a beautiful shade of violet and of considerable size.

Their roots are not long and tangled as one might suppose, but short and thickish with blunt ends. Sometimes they resemble coral with short branches. On examination these roots are found to have a larger number of fungi than any plants of the other two groups. They are full to overflowing and for a very good reason. The Saprophyte, living only on rotted humus, is not only fed by its root fungus but is also freed from the necessity of doing any assimilation of its own and so it can dispense with foliage. That is in broad outline as much as one can say about saprophytes here. For want of space we must omit any detailed description of how the different orchids get their food. The subject is far too extensive. Those who wish for further information should consult Professor Burgeff's books.

Those, however, who would like to know more about Saprophytic orchids, are recommended to study the bird's nest orchid *Neottia nidus avis* L. which is a native of European beech woods and the rare species of *Coralliorrhiza* and *Limodorum*. Mention might also be made of another pale (flowered) variety, the yellow bird's nest, *Monotropa hypopitys* L. of the *Pirolaceae* family which is often met with in the European fir forests. It will serve as an example to show that it is not only orchids which choose to live on humus.

EPIPHYTIC ORCHIDS (Living on trees)
(Greek epi = on, above: phyton = plant)

The epiphytic group is the largest and most important one, for it provides us with the finest representatives of the orchid world, and therefore merits our closest attention. Their habitat is mainly at the top of gigantic tropical trees. Here they grow luxuriantly 150-200 feet above the ground. It is impossible to see them from below or even to have any inkling of their presence. Year in, year out, they defy the storms and tropical weather, clinging fast with their clasping roots to the branches.

It is generally agreed, and with a fair amount of probability, that the plants which now grow on trees formerly had their habitat in the soil in the days when tropical forests were thinner and lighter than now.

The struggle for sunlight, their source of life, did not arise among the smaller plants growing on the ground until these forests became denser and more shut in. The stronger ones gained the upper hand as living conditions became more and more unfavourable to the smaller ones. The existence of the latter was threatened in the darkness that prevailed on the ground. The tropical forests attracted an increasing amount of heavy rain by their thickness and extent, and are sometimes called rain or mist forests. The air was thereby saturated with the humidity which enabled orchids, particularly the epiphytic type, to transfer to the trees.

The latter may perhaps at first have settled on the lower parts of the trunks and thus, aided by the wind, have increased their powers of scattering their seed upwards. The undergrowth, consisting of creepers and other climbing plants, grew higher and more tangled and compelled the epiphytic orchids to climb still higher till they got to the very top of the tallest trees whose foliage also protected them from the scorching rays of the equatorial sun. The orchids which live in company with many other epiphytic plants such as various kinds of ferns, bromeliads, araceae, cacti, lichens, mosses etc., grow thickly on branches, in the fork of branches and wherever else they can get a foothold. They must, therefore, be reckoned as plants requiring shade and this fact must be taken into account when cultivating them.

As a rule the small modest orchids establish themselves more densely, whereas the larger ones with the magnificent flowers are scattered or appear in colonies. But they all have to adapt themselves to conditions and develop the corresponding organs. We shall go further into this adaptation when we describe these separately.

As regards nourishment, the epiphytic orchids have a masterly way of surviving on the absolute minimum, thanks to their unique adaptability, for the layer of humus which is available in their lofty position is thin and meagre, and though we may think they are half-starved they yet manage to assert themselves and fulfil their function through the changing seasons of the year and produce their magic blooms.

The epiphytic orchids growing in their natural state are more dependent for food on their mycorrhiza than are cultivated ones. Professor Burgeff has shown in his book *Germination of Orchid Seeds* that there are digestive cells in orchid roots where the fungi are broken down and partly digested to serve as food.

An example from the animal world shows still more clearly in how large a measure fungi can contain albumen and other important foodstuffs. The leaf-cutting ants in the tropics cut up leaves of the Cecropia trees into small pieces and carry them held over their heads like shields with a kind of goose step to their anthill. Here the fragments of leaf are piled and made to ferment and then they are inoculated with the appropriate fungus. In this way the ants provide themselves with a supply of fungus which then serves as nourishment on which to feed and bring up the young ones. They work by instinct of course, but surely nature would not have made them act in this way if the vital chemicals they needed for their physical development were not contained in the fungi.

The symbiosis of fungus and orchid is to be thought of in the same way. The fungi act as a kind of nurse. They have the power of pushing their mycelia out of the orchid root and spreading rapidly into the surrounding substratum of humus where bacteria are at work breaking down organic matter and changing it.

This process of change is helped and accelerated by the prevailing sultry atmosphere, produced by a combination of heat and humidity in the air. The air is constantly being replenished with moisture from the downpours of rain which occur once or twice a day in these regions.

Presumably the mycelia of the fungus growing freely in their natural state either induct the food into the orchid in a palatable form or provide the food themselves. We do not yet know whether the bacteria in the humus play any part or, if so, what it is. The question of how wild orchids get their food is still awaiting a clear answer.

An equally important process common to the life of orchids and all other greenstuffs and closely connected with feeding is the assimilation of carbon. It goes on by day only in the chlorophyll cells which take in carbonic acid gas from the air, and oxygen so vital to man and beast is combined with it and given off by the plant.

Through this assimilation of carbon the plants acquire the strength for the building up of their parts. After it has been made available i.e., by being turned into sugar, it is carried by night from the cells of the leaves, the actual organs of assimilation, to the places where it is needed for growth. If need be, it is stored up in certain places and held in reserve.

Assimilation is not the same as breathing. This latter goes on concurrently and continually through all the parts of the plant. Assimilation begins only with the return of daylight. Till then the cells of the leaves must remain empty so that there is room for the next day's work.

The layer of humus can form but a shallow depth on branches. It is only when they are thickly colonised and the orchid roots are interlaced with those of a number of other epiphytes growing alongside them that such a layer can be formed at all. Leaves, petals, bits of other plants, remains of fruit etc., fall from the treetops on to the branches and provide new sources of nourishment. Rain water, too, has to contribute to the enrichment of feeding matter by bringing down many salts, some of them crystalline, that have been exuded from the leaves of the trees. Perhaps, too, the nitrogenous excrement of tropical birds and tree-climbing animals may play a larger part than we suspect.

As against this, the tree-growing orchids in the sub-tropical regions find themselves in much less favourable circumstances. In the first place, they have to sustain a longer dry period in which there is no rain at all and then the forest areas are not so dense and the heavy rains are spread out more unevenly. Further, the orchids appear not in groups but isolated, so exposing them more to the drying action of the wind and the sun, whose rays manage to reach them occasionally. On account of the milder temperature and small quantity of moisture in the air, the waste material does not rot so quickly as in the tropics. For this reason and because there are no close colonies of plants on the branches, no humus can be retained, and the orchids are attached to the smooth branches. It is scarcely possible to say in detail how they get their nourishment; it is certain that they are skilled in the art of getting a living!

We know that orchids of the sub-tropical regions protect themselves against too much desiccation by a kind of armour plating: that is, by a tough outer skin which turns their leavers and stems into store-houses of food and water. Many of them have reduced their leaf surface to an absolute minimum in order to avoid too much evaporation. The leaves are often small and narrow, cylindrical and of a succulent nature, being fleshy, full of sap and with a tough texture. Other orchids help them-out by shedding their leaves in the dry season.

To balance this their pseudo-bulbs, which are round or oval in shape, bulge with an abundance of food and water. Even their roots are strikingly limited. For the most part they lack the thick, spongy, aerial roots of the tropical tree-dwellers; in fact there are relatively few strong wiry clasping roots among them.

This remarkable habit of living and flourishing in those precarious conditions enables us to understand better why tree-dwelling orchids can survive in artificial cultivation only when the soil is made almost exclusively from fern roots and moss taken from bogs.

CHAPTER III

BIOLOGY AND MORPHOLOGY OF THE PLANT ORGANS

ROOTS

The main task of the roots is to provide the plant with water and the essential foods dissolved in it. They are specially designed and developed for this purpose. We know them mostly as soft white threads that are easily broken, and it is astonishing how these tender organs succeed in pushing through the soil, assuring the food supply and enabling the plant to maintain an erect position. Their inner anatomical structure is in itself a work of art, in which processes and forces operate.

The roots of orchids are particularly distinguishable, especially those of the epiphytes to which we must give special attention. The roots of the terrestrial type differ widely from other plants in that they are not branched, but solitary. They are also on the whole thicker and sometimes shorter.

Among the tree-dwelling orchids we must distinguish between clasping or climbing roots and aerial roots. The clasping kind serves to anchor the plant to the tree in the first place, and in the second place to take in water and food, whereas the aerial roots—as the name implies— take in moisture from the air as they wave to and fro in the breezes.

In contradistinction to the clasping roots, which may also be wholly or partly free in the air, the aerial-rooted variety appears mostly higher up the stem and when they find a point of contact with branches they take root and give stability to the very long stem.

Occasionally nests of roots are formed out of the laterals of the clasping roots. These lateral roots grow bolt upright, branch out horizontally in all directions and behave like sharp thorns. They are interspersed with soft hair-like roots, such as can sometimes be seen on luxuriantly growing kinds of *Catasetum*. This curious natural arrangement presumably serves to catch deposits from the tops of trees and also to make humus.

The aerial-roots are mostly thick like the clasping roots of the sturdier kinds of orchids. In some cases they are as thick as a little finger, mostly round in shape and white or greenish in colour. Many orchids also have flat ribbon-like spreading roots, which are rich in chlorophyll e.g., some types of *Phalaenopsis* and the rare leafless orchids, whose roots are green. They take on the assimilation instead of the leaves.

The anatomical structure of the roots of epiphytic orchids permits of a rough microscopic examination, from which we ascertain that the real root lies embedded in a relatively thick loose tissue called velamen. In its dry state, velamen consists of cells with a good-sized mesh which can easily be compressed like a sponge. Only with the help of this sponge-like velamen can the aerial-roots suck in moisture from the air and convey it to the plant.

We gather from this that epiphytic orchids must be surrounded all the time with a very moist atmosphere and in a correspondingly high temperature. It is a matter of life or death to them for in too dry an atmosphere the aerial roots would shrivel up and their essential function thereby be prevented. This applies with the greatest emphasis to tropical orchids.

PSEUDO-BULBS — STEMS

It is essential to distinguish between

      (a) orchids that have no stem,

      (b) those that have a pseudo-bulb,

and (c) those with a single perennial stem.

All bush-orchids and those that have no bulb, like members of the *Paphiopedilum* family, belong to the stemless variety.

The second group, having a pseudo-bulb for their stem, include the host of sympodial orchids, to which belong the genera

Cattleya, Coelogyne, Laelia, Dendrobium, Lycaste, Epidendrum, etc., to mention only a few.

The third group comprises all single-stem orchids, such as *Angraecum, Vanda, Phalaenopsis,* etc.

There are many varieties of pseudo-bulbs. All the transitional forms are to be found from the short round through the oval, cylindrical and spindle shaped to the ones with a long stem. This stem is to a greater or lesser extent flat-sided. In addition it may have one or many sections. These may be smoothly wrapped in relatively thin sheaths which in the dry state are like parchment or thin skin.

The stems are at the same time leaf-bearing in a variety of arrangements.

With the pseudo-bulb stems the leaves are either single or there are several together at the top end. With the single stem variety, which is often covered with leaves from bottom to top, these are mostly arranged around the stem in alternating rows of two, or more or less close together in a spiral.

At the base of the sympodial orchid's stem there are always two eyes one on either side. The young shoot, which becomes the pseudo-bulb, sprouts from these eyes. As a rule only one such bulb is formed each year, but with strong plants, or for some other reason, both eyes may sprout at the same time. This frequently occurs with the strong Cattleya plants.

If the two eyes meet with anything that causes them to die off before the new growth, no further shoots can be expected from this particular pseudo-bulb. If there is not another, older stem with a healthy eye the plant has become valueless because it can no longer either develop or flower.

The eyes therefore are very precious and should be protected carefully from harm. Damage can arise from a knock caused by careless handling. Newly grown eyes that already protrude are especially liable to break off, while young ones are easily destroyed by pests. The plants must therefore not be neglected. The harm done by pests is far too great to be overlooked. So the destruction of pests at their very first appearance must be the priority rule for the orchid grower.

LEAVES

Leaves are extraordinarily important. They have to prepare the carbon compounds needed for the development of the plant's structure. They also provide for the evaporation of water from the body of the plant by their stomata. These and the continual alimentation through the roots regulate the circulation of moisture in the plant. This rotation occurs automatically. It works more quickly in great heat and more slowly as the temperature falls. In winter it almost stops.

For this purpose the leaves have received suitable forms and properties. The shape of this leaf surface is capable of incredible variations. They can be differentiated into round without subdivisions, oval, egg-shaped, lanceolated, tapered, sub-divided, denticulated, serrated, and so on.

The colour is usually green owing to the chlorophyll. Occasionally, however, variegated leaves appear and are regarded as an adornment of the plant.

Orchid leaves are always entire and fairly simple in form. They are chiefly long, tapering or tongue-shaped with parallel veins. This is one of the reasons for including them among the monocotyledons.

A further proof is this single cotyledon. It is scarcely visible to the amateur eye for it can be seen only in the embryo form and then only with a magnifying-glass.

As there is no rigid regularity in nature, we find orchids with the heart-shaped leaves and pinnate veins that are peculiar to the dicotyledons. The leaves are joined to the stem with or without stalk. They may be short or of varying length. There are great differences in texture as well, passing by stages from hard and leathery to soft and pulpy. The leaves may be light or dark green in colour or a mixture of both. They may be brightly marked in yellowish, whitish and a dark green colour like marble or like the squares of a chessboard, as, for example in the tropical *Paphiopediliums*. Yet others are veritable jewels of colour, with their gold, silver and copper-like veins on a velvet green or dark velvet green background. The best-known species belonging to this category are the *Anoectochilus, Haemaria* and the glorious *Macodes petola,* which is unique.

Most orchids have perennial leaves which they keep for years. They are technically known as evergreen-orchids. A considerable number, however, keep their leaves for only a short time. The leaves die off regularly every year. They are green only during growth and the plants lose their foliage at the beginning of the dry season.

INFLORESCENCE

In orchids the inflorescence is, in some cases, single-stemmed, but mostly it takes the form of a raceme and is more rarely paniculate.

The single flowering stem, also called a scape, bears one or two blossoms. If there are three or more blossoms on the scape, each on its own stalk, we talk of a raceme. A raceme becomes a panicule when the scape branches out and the flowers grow out, each on its own stalk, both on the main stem and on the branch stems.

The flower stems are either terminal (acranthous) or lateral (pleuranthous). Flowers at the end of single stems often emerge from a large sheath e.g. the *Cattleyas* and *Laelias*; whereas the pleuranthous flowers grow out of the axil of the leaf as with the *Angraecum* and *Vanda.* The scape can vary greatly in length, from quite short to as long as six feet in the *Oncidium.*

Normally, the flower stems are either perpendicular, bent to one side or the other, or they arch right over. In extreme cases some orchids let their flowers hang upside down by allowing the stem to hang rigidly down in the opposite direction. The stems are either bare, covered with soft hairs or provided with large or small sheaths, which vary in their closeness together. In the case of racemes and panicles we often find so called bracts or protective leaves at the base of the stalk.

FLOWERS

All organs of the plant are adjusted to fulfil the purpose of propagation. They are developed and built up accordingly. This development took such fascinating and beautiful forms and people were so delighted with them that the best plants were cultivated. Ever since plants have been classified the chief distinguishing mark by which the families, genera and species were determined and arranged, has been the flowers. It is still the most important character today.

Engler's system divides all flowering plants into two classes according to the number of their cotyledons. Those which have only one cotyledon belong to the class of Monocotyledoneae, whereas all others, with two cotyledons, belong to the Dicotyledon class. A further mark of distinction is found in the veins of the leaves. In Monocotyledons the veins are usually parallel, in dicotyledons they are pinnate.

Our orchids belong to the monocotyledon class for the above reasons and are therefore closely related to the *Liliaceae* family.

The structure of the orchid flower is more complicated than that of any other flowering plant, and it is endowed in addition with lavish embellishments, noble forms and brilliant colours. Some are remarkable for their unusual and odd shapes which sometimes become fantastically grotesque, of for their colouring: yellowy green, dark brown, dark purple-red or black and red. They look like masks. They are decorated with excrescences and appendages of all kinds which are rather difficult to distinguish and not always easy to describe. There is an extraordinary variation in the size of the flowers, ranging from one up to twenty centimetres. Their petals may be soft transparent and scented while others, especially the odd shaped ones, have a wax-like consistency.

Scent does not play a very large part in orchids but there are some which have a pleasing smell and others with a rather strong, almost offensive, smell, as in the Stanhopeas.

The sexual organs of the orchid flower are particularly complicated. It is not so easy for the observer to find the anther and the stigma as it is with our native wild flowers. The anther is either hidden by the thick lip or it lies in a cavity at the end of the column called a clinandrium.

CHAPTER IV

THE STRUCTURE OF THE ORCHID FLOWER

In order to get a thorough knowledge and understanding of the parts of the orchid flower, let us take a closer look at diagram 1, A B & C.

Fig. 1

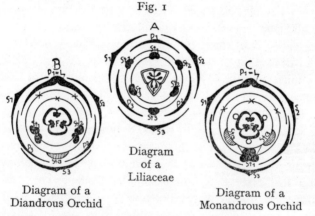

Diagram of a
Diandrous Orchid

Diagram
of a
Liliaceae

Diagram of a
Monandrous Orchid

S = sepals. P = petals. F = ovary with placentae. P₁ = L = labellum
St = stamens. Sta = staminodes.

The diagrams show a cross-section cut through a bud that is still closed. The flowers of the monocotyledenous plants, to which orchids belong, are usually ternate as can be seen in Diagram A of the Liliaceae, that is to say all the parts are in threes and show the perfect type of bloom in the monocotyledon class.

In the diagram of a lily we also find in the outer circle three sepals grouped round the centre, in the second three petals, in the third and fourth three stamens each. In the fifth and last we see the pistil with three stigmas and three carpels.

If we now look at diagrams B and C we find that triple arrangement upset. In diagram B we find only two, and in diagram C only one stamen. The missing ones can be partly made out under a microscope as stunted growths or retrograde formations, the so-called staminodes.

As all living things succumb to the changes of time, so may plants in the course of long periods of time show changes in growth which rank as concrescent or retrograde formations or possibly even as new structures. These changes are probably set going by shocks sustained in violent weather conditions and, in certain circumstances, by eruptions on the earth's surface that at the same time liberate gases which may have a stimulating effect on the plants. From scientific experiments we know that cold, alkaloids (plant poisons) and also radiation of ultra sound waves cause transformations in the generating cells of plants which can lead on to the development of mutations.

We must picture to ourselves the development of orchids in a similar way. We have shown that they belong to the monocotyledon class by the presence of the three sepals and petals. They differ from the *Liliaceae,* to which they are most closely related, by the smaller number of their stamens. Another difference is the union of the pistil with the stamens with the column thus joining the male and female organs. Considerable differences are also to be found in the position of the ovaries. In lilies the ovary is above the base of the flower. It is usually three-celled, whereas in orchids the ovary is always below the base of the flower and is usually one-celled.

The French botanist, A. L. de Jussieu, who died in Paris in 1836, established the family *Orchidaceae* in consideration of the differences in flower structure. The name is derived from the genus *Orchis* which grow in Europe. The last syllable, *daceae,* means plants, so *orchidaceae* is the same as orchids plants.

As we have already seen from diagrams B & C orchids have two typical and entirely different flower forms which we must get to know more intimately.

In diagram B we have the diandrous type with two fertile stamens. All diandrous orchids have been incorporated in Pfister's system under the title First sub-family *Diandreae,* Group 1, *Cypripedilinae.* He established a second sub-family for the monandrous orchids, (which have only one stamen as shown in diagram C).

DIANDROUS FLOWERS (Fig. 2)

In the second drawing we have a diagram of a diandrous flower which, as a superficial inspection shows, differs considerably in structure from the monandrous flower sketched in diagram 3.

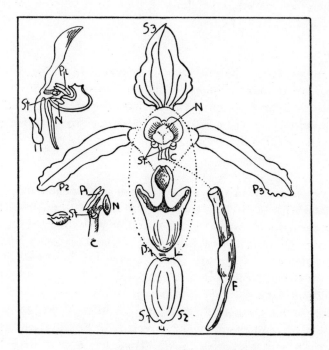

Fig. 2. Diandrous Flower (diagramatic)
S 1-3 (1 and 2 united) = sepals. P 2-3 = petals. Pl = L = labellum.
C = column. N = 3-partite stigma. St = anther. F = ovary. Pl =
staminode (disc)

The most prominent feature of this type is the lip called the labellum. It is common to all four genera of the *Cypripedilinae* and is shoe-shaped. Although the labellum in diagram B is directly above the stem in the second circle, later on when the flower is fully open it is below it, having turned through 180 degrees.

This turning, known as resupination, sometimes results in a twisted ovary. Striking, too, in this type of flower is the way the two side-sepals have grown together into one, now situated behind the labellum. They are rarely found separate. The dorsal sepal, which looks like a helmet held above the column, is known as the standard.

The style, called the column in orchids, is likewise basically different in the two types.

Sepals

The upper sepal—the standard—may take many different ovoid shapes, or it may be short, round or broad. In addition it is brightly coloured, often with fascinating embellishments. The lower united ones are mostly an unobtrusive green. It varies in size and is oval in shape.

Petals

The two lateral petals are always similar in shape and colour. In common with their class, they are also subject to modifications. They can be narrower or broader and of very different lengths, reaching 50 centimetres in a few cases. They may also be ribbon-shaped. They are either horizontal or they incline inwards towards each other or outwards away from each other. Sometimes they are bent downwards in a more or less elegant fashion or hang smoothly down to one side. There are many different colours: green, yellowy green, light brown, dark brown, also green with a reddish brown. Their upper edge may have a lot of pretty little black warts covered with hairs.

Labellum

The lower middle petal which forms the labellum always has a curious shape like a shoe. Its size, colour and form vary with each species. It rarely happens that two lips are alike. One can only be amazed at the variety of form and colour. Nature reveals herself as a great artist. The lip may be mottled red and white like the whole flower. More often it is of a different colour, brown to dark brown, yellowy green with a network of veins, or all shades of buff and dark purple. The edge of the lip is mostly smooth, rarely incurved. The genus *Phragmopedilum* is the only one distinguished in this way.

Column

The column in the fifth circle of diagram B rests on the ovary. It is to a certain extent the continuation of it. In form and arrangement it is quite different from the column in monandrous orchids (diagram C). The single stamen in the third circle has been transformed into a staminode, resting like a disc on the forked column. This disc is shaped like a kidney and is a characteristic of the diandrous orchid.

Behind this scutiform plate and concealed from sight lies the female organ, the tripartite stigma on the end of the column. Slightly below the stigma, on either side of the column, are the male organs arranged in the form of two small bowls filled with a sticky mass of pollen. The lip is united with the base of the column.

Monandrous Flowers (Fig. 3)

As the term monandrous (lit. one-man) indicates, this type of flower differs sharply in character from the diandrous by having only one stamen. But the column and adjoining lip have also undergone an important change and it will be interesting to examine this form of flower more closely (diagram B).

Sepals

All three sepals in the monandrous flower are separate and fairly similar in shape and colour, particularly the two side ones which are always exactly alike. They are slightly bent on the side nearest to the middle sepal because of their sloping position.

Petals

The two upper petals—the lower one acting as the lip—are mostly broader than the sepals or similar in form. Often both are considerably broader and their edges may be beautifully waved in a decorative way, scalloped or denticulated as, for example, with various *Cattleyas* but they all have the same colour.

Labellum

The labellum of monandrous orchids is freer and consequently it is more beautiful, more scented and less unusual in its varied forms than the shoe-shaped one of the diandrous flower. Usually it has three lobes. The two side ones are more or less wrapped round the flower column like a tube or paper bag. The front lobe

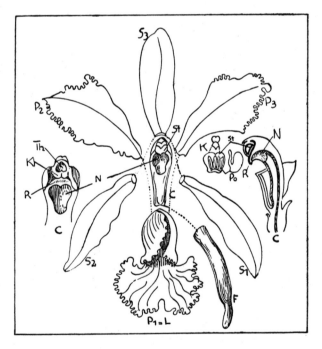

Fig. 3. Monandrous Flower
S 1-3 = sepals. Pl-3 = petals. Pl = labellum. C = column. N = stigma. K = cap (deciduous). St = anther. Po = pollinium. R = rostellum. Kl = clinandrium. Th = theca. F = ovary.

shows extraordinary changes in size. The formation of the lip is looser than in the diandrous flower and it often shows all kinds of pretty decorations such as a jointed front lobe, horns, appendages and other growths. The lobe is variously divided; not just once or twice, but even three times.

A good example of the three-jointed lip is seen in the *Stanhopea* flowers. The lower one is called the hypochil, the middle one the mesochil and the upper one the epichil. As if that were not decorative enough the edge of the lip takes a hand. In simple cases it is smooth but it can also be found beautifully waved, scalloped or finely fimbriated.

The beauty of its colouring is at times heightened by brighter and paler shades than are to be found on the lip of the diandrous orchid. It is very striking and can be recognised by its stronger colours and spots of varying size, which may be different in colour from other parts of the flower. There is a good reason for this. The front lobe of the labellum serves as a landing platform for flying insects. Cleverly adapted for this purpose, it grows out horizontally in front of the column.

Column

Compared with the column of the diandrous group, this one is remarkable for its slender and simple shape. It is well represented in sketch 3 by one of the largest flowers of its group—a *Cattleya* flower. Individual kinds naturally vary in length and texture.

Although the column is the most important part of the flower, owing to its supporting both organs of reproduction, anyone who was not aware of it would scarcely see anything of such organs on the column even with close observation. Not even a yellow anther is visible as it is in the flowers of other plants. Only after the closest scrutiny does one notice a small cavity in the front wall of the column. That is the stigma. Just above it, let into the head of the column, lies the male organ with the anther, which is sometimes covered by a cap that opens and, on being touched, shuts down again.

Stigmas

The stigma of diandrous flowers develops normally. It has three lobes where the monandrous have only succeeded in forming two. A dividing partition grows out of the third lobe, also called the rostellum. It is shaped like a tongue and divides the stigma from the anther.

In most cases the surface of the stigma precipitates a sticky substance designed to hold the pollen deposited on it. In other cases it may be papillose, i.e., the surface may be thickly covered with short hair-like papillae to hold the pollen more firmly.

The stigma needs a direct connection with the ovary (egg-sack). For this purpose there is a tube through the middle of the column from about the centre of the stigma right into the seed compartments of the ovary.

Rostellum

The rostellum, or small beak, which varies in length and looks like a tongue, rises in front of the upper rim of the stigma and so prevents the pollen, that is, the pollinia, from falling on its own stigma. In the main, orchids are cross-pollinated i.e. they need the help of certain insects. Self-fertilisation occurs more rarely. It is mostly found in the smaller varieties known as botanical orchids. The rostellum serves another purpose. On its upper surface it carries a sticky mass and the stalks of the pollinia; only when the pollinia have reached a state of maturity can this be removed from the rostellum like a fine skin. In its middle part the rostellum is shorter or longer according to the length of the small stalk called a stipe. The sticky substance is mostly found on the pointed end in the small notch.

Pollen and Pollinia

Pollen is the name given to the yellow dust in the flower which is still found granular and free in the diandrous orchids. Dust is hardly the appropriate word because it is really dough-like and sticky.

The arrangement is quite different, however, in the monandrous flowers. There the pollen is stored in pockets (sacks) and these in their turn form, with the aid of ingenious appendages, an apparatus like a rocket which reaches its most perfect form in the *Catasetum* flowers and is something like a projectile. These flowers are thus able to release the pollen explosively.

This apparatus is called an anther or stamen or pollen-sack. It is also known as pollium. There are always several of these pollinia stuck together and the number in the anther varies with the species. It may be 2, 4, 8, 16 or more.

Anthers

The pollen lies within the anther which often has a fairly complicated structure, especially when the pollinium is provided with a tiny stalk which, in its turn, rests on the centre of a sticky disc, mostly round in shape. The stalk with the pollium stands straight up, but at the point of contact with the disc it can move in any direction like a ball-joint.

The anther also undergoes many modifications in its structure. Not only one but two pollinia grains side by side may possibly be found on the stalk. Both then give the effect of two auricles. The two pollinia may, however, have each its own stalk resting on one enlarged sticky disc. In the simplest case, the anther has only one stalk which, as it leaves the cavity in the column where it lies embedded, gets its sticky matter from the rostellum, so as to be able to attach itself to the insect's body.

Both parts of the fertilising organs, male and female, are found together in the column of the flower. Consequently orchids must be reckoned as belonging mainly to the bi-sexual or hermaphrodite order of plants. The representatives of the genera *Catasetum* and *Cycnoches* are, however, exceptions. Plants of one sex only, with all male or all female flowers, appear in both species. Plants are also found with unisexual flowers, male or female, in one head of blooms. We shall go further into the relationship between the flowers of the genus *Catasetum* when we come to the individual description of the special species.

Ovary

The rather thickened ovary, which varies in length, is easily recognisable by the fact that it undergoes a reduction in size as it passes into the thinner leaf-stalk. It is composed of the three carpels which are always to be found in the fifth circle of the flower (see diagrams p. 33), where their three sutures meet on the ovary; the edges of their leaves stick up somewhat into the capsule and form the placentae. In this case we are dealing with a one-celled capsule. If the edges grow further in, so as to form three partitions, we have an ovary, with three capsules.

By far the greatest number of orchids have a one-celled ovary; e.g., all the monandrous orchids and the diandrous genera *Cypripedilum* and *Paphiopedilum*. On the other hand, the diandrous genera *Selenipedilum* and *Phragmopedilum* always have three compartments.

The female cells are on the placentae. They are the embryos from which the seeds come after fertilisation. By the gradual development of the seed the ovary becomes the fruit and finally the dry dehiscent seed-capsule. The fruits are club-shaped and vary greatly in size in accordance with the great wealth of varieties.

The capsules hold an enormous number of seeds. Those of the small orchids alone shelter tens of thousands. Medium-sized varieties hold some hundred thousands and the largest fruit capsules several millions. As the seed-grains are very small, large quantities can be produced and find room in the capsules.

The seeds develop very slowly till the fruit is mature. In the small species they take six or more months; in larger species eight to twelve months or even longer. *Paphiopedilum* species, for example, require eleven to twelve months.

Seed Dispersal

The ripe capsule of the orchid releases its seeds by tearing open the sutures lengthwise and spreading out the three carpels which have thereby been liberated. Smaller capsules are emptied by the shaking of the wind. Larger ones have hair-like catapults inside them which help to propel the seeds into the air. The wind does the rest. In their natural habitat, therefore, orchid seeds are scattered by the wind. That is why the seed is so tiny. It consists either of light grains as fine as dust or like chaff, which can be blown away by the slightest breeze. The vanilla species are an exception. Their seeds are somewhat larger and form a doughy mass in the capsule.

The dispersal of the seeds by the wind is obviously suited to the epiphytic orchids. And we can now understand why there is such mass production of seeds, for only a small number can be fortunate enough to reach a suitable spot on a branch that provides all the conditions needed for new orchids to grow. By far the largest number are uselessly destroyed. It is, as it were, a kind of stabilisation device of nature which allows so many seeds to be produced.

Pollination, Fertilisation

Orchid flowers are dependent on outside pollination which is done by certain insects, such as bees. Certain kinds of these bees are to be found overseas, but we know next to nothing about these guests of the orchid. This is due to the impossibility of observing the insects at work in the tree tops of the mist-laden forests where the orchids live in seclusion.

The structure and arrangement of the flowers act as a tremerdous inducement. Their profusion of beautiful colour and shining light, their lavish and varied adornments, their noble form and even on occasion their scent, all serve to attract their guests, who indeed find a well-covered table. There are flowers with spurs containing honey and nectar. Where there are no spurs they are exuded at the base of the flower. Occasionally, saccharic acid is found instead of nectar. Other orchids have so-called nutrient tissue containing albumen to offer, in shape like hairs. In this way the insects find their food served up in great variety. These enticing baits are so arranged in the flower that the insect has to pass the sexual organs of the column so that it can dust the stigma with the pollen it has brought with it and take on another load. In order to find out the sequence of this process of pollination, let us follow the tracks of an insect.

Let us suppose a bumble-bee is on its way to collect nectar. It scents the perfume of the flower. This pleases the bee and it goes after the flower. Once it is near enough to see the orchid, the eye takes over the direction from the sense of smell. The bee finds unerringly the place where the flower is growing and lands on the lip of a bloom. Let us say it is a *Cattleya* flower which has a number of blooms in a spike. Guided by the scent, it proceeds to the column at the bottom of which the nectar is exuded. On its way thither it squeezes past the stigma cavity right into the throat. While doing this it scrapes off on to the stigma one of the pollinia hanging on its body, which it has possibly brought with it after visiting a flower of the same kind. That completes the pollination.

On the way in, the pollinia above the stigma are covered by the anther and cannot be touched. But on the way out from the bottom of the flower, the bee pushes up the protruding tongue of the rostellum. At the same moment the rostellum excretes some sticky substance which is stroked off on to the bee's back and carried away. Concurrently with this, the anther is pushed open by the upward thrust of the tongue of the rostellum. The pollinia, emerge and cling to the sticky substance on the bee's back so that they can be stroked off in the next flower and thus maintain the rhythm of pollination.

Fertilisation sets in after this. The bees transfer the pollinia, small parts of which are used for fertilising, to the surface of the stigma where they develop into elongated pollen-tubes which push their way through the channel in the column to the interior of the ovary. The tissue of the pollen-tube contains the male germ cells which now come into contact with the female egg-cell in the seed placenta and coalesce.

Fertilisation is not complete till this merger of both sex-cells which pollination initiates has taken place, for each is a different process, separated in plants, whereas in animals mating and fertilisation are one and the same thing. Activity then starts inside the ovary. The seeds slowly develop from the female egg-cells which can be noticed from outside by the swelling of the ovary. This ceases when maturity is reached.

After pollination, the splendour of the flower quickly fades. Next morning at the latest all the petals will have drooped and faded or will have fallen off, as example in the *Paphiopedilum* species. For this reason those who cultivate *Cymbidiums* for cut flowers fear the bees for they pollinate their blooms, which then quickly fade. If these unwelcome guests are not kept away, the owner stands to lose his livelihood.

CHAPTER V

PROPAGATION OF ORCHIDS

Sexual Reproduction

To understand sexual reproduction is to understand the natural way that all plants derived from seed are propagated and gardeners from their experience developed their own methods, especially with the more delicate plants.

But so far as the propagation of orchids from seed is concerned, it was as we have indicated, a long time before successful methods were discovered, and these go far beyond anything that is usually done in horticulture.

At first the symbiotic method was developed, but it proved far too difficult for the horticulturist to succeed with it alone. The asymbiotic method, which grew out of the symbiotic, made the work of sowing fairly reliable. It is now being practised with the greatest success. As the symbiotic method is no longer of great importance, we shall say only what is absolutely necessary about it.

Symbiotic Sowing

Although the symbiotic method is the closer to nature, it is the more difficult of the two. The mycorrhiza can be isolated from the cell tissues of the root only with the aid of a microscope. In addition one must always have available pure cultures of the appropriate fungus for inoculating the seeds.

These two complicated conditions are abolished by the asymbiotic method. As all the procedures in both methods are in effect the same, we shall describe only the asymbiotic one in more detail to avoid repetition. In any case the necessity for absolutely sterile work demands a laboratory with scientific apparatus and the necessary knowledge.

ASYMBIOTIC SOWING

After the establishment of the asymbiotic method in America, it was soon taken up in Europe and it has proved the most suitable for practical purposes as well as the most favourable economically.

The asymbiotic method, as its name implies, dispenses with fungus; by it the fungus can be replaced with sugar (cane, beet, fruit or grape).

In every process sterilisation plays a decisive rôle and success depends entirely on carrying it out with painstaking care. Above all one must sterilise everything that is used and keep it sterilised until the work is finished, in order to preserve the cultures from disease caused by parasitic fungi. One must not therefore use flower-pots or other earthenware vessels when sowing, but glass tubes in the form of test-tubes and cylindrical bulbs. There must also be a steriliser available. According to Thomale's *Orchids,* it can be replaced, if need be, by a simple cooking apparatus.

Agar Agar, a product of seaweed used in science for the culture of bacteria, serves as a culture medium for the seeds. It is boiled for one or two minutes in distilled water and cooled down to a gelatinous mass. Besides the prescribed quantities of sugar, a series of chemical agents in liquid form are added to the mass after being carefully and exactly measured out by prescription. Standard formulae were tested and established for general use e.g., by Burgeff, Knudson and other. They give the quantities of the individual nutritive salts. These should be weighed out only by an apothecary's scales as the smallest units of weight involved. After that the sterilised test-tubes are filled with the culture media and immediately closed with a wad of cotton wool which has been passed over a bunsen burner. After they have been put through the steriliser, the prepared test-tubes remain slightly tilted until the agar has set.

SOWING ON CULTURE MEDIUM

Sowing is best done on the following day. After the seed has been sterilised in a chloride of lime solution, it is sown on the media with a platinum needle and the tube is immediately reclosed with the cotton-wool wad. Needle and wad must be regularly sterilized. If a boiling apparatus is available, all the work is carried out in the steam. The hands must then be protected by rubber gloves.

The receptacles containing the cultures are now kept either in an incubator on wooden stands made to fit them, or better still in a glass case with sliding doors in a greenhouse. The prevailing moisture in the atmosphere prevents the medium from drying quickly, though it increases the danger of mildew getting in. In this case the cotton wool must again be made safe by a parchment or cellophane cap.

25° Centigrade is the most favourable temperature for the development of the seedlings and it should be kept as constant as possible in diffused light from which direct rays from the sun are excluded.

PRICKING OFF AND TRANSPLANTING

If all possible sources of error have been avoided successfully, the seedlings will be ready for pricking out after an average of six months. Variations in individual genera and species must, of course, be taken into account.

The first pricking out takes place usually when the culture medium is exhausted. This new procedure follows the same rhythm as sowing did formerly; but now it is the tiny seedlings which have to be transplanted; so once again they must be transferred with a platinum needle to a similar medium and sealed in test-tubes with cotton-wool stoppers as when first sown and all this must be done in an absolutely sterile manner. The conditions of environment as regards light and warmth remain the same.

Sometimes disturbances in the course of cultivation may make certain intermediary measures necessary. Such is the case, for example, when the nutritive value of the solution is used up too soon and results in stunted growth in the seedlings. You can then add to the nutritive substances and compensate them by means of a syringe injecting through the wool stopper the same basic solution (see Thomale).

By this process you avoid the more troublesome method of transplanting, which, however, cannot be avoided when undesirable fungi appear in spite of all precautionary measures.

If, in the meantime, the seedlings, which at first cling on by root hairs, have become so strong as to have developed roots and two or three leaves, then pricking out can be carried out. The small plants are now finally released from captivity in test-tubes, so that they can get accustomed to freedom. A new span of life, as it were, begins for them, one which requires a different approach from those who cultivate them. They are first planted in peat in seed pans. Only clean pots must be used. If they are new ones they must first be soaked in clean water.

This poor substratum of sterile peat, which may be mixed with charcoal and river-sand, is particularly recommended because of a harmful pest which is dangerous for the roots of the young plants and avoids peat. It is the larva of the "Sadfly" (*Sciara tritici* Cog).

When the small plants have been transferred with the usual wooden dibber to the pots which are filled to about one-third with clean sherds, with the sterilized peat mould on top of them, they are put back into the incubator or into clean glass cases in the greenhouse.

FURTHER CULTIVATION

After the potting stage, rearing the seedlings assumes more the character of gardening. The atmosphere of the place where they are growing, especially if it is a section of a greenhouse, must, during the first transition period, show a high degree of moisture maintained at an even temperature of 25° Centigrade. The moisture should be produced by a vaporiser or hand syringe without wetting the plants at first. After about two weeks they are first lightly sprayed until gradually they are brought to the stage of being syringed.

In the course of ten to twelve weeks, according to the strength of the young plants, a further transplantation becomes necessary. In cases where the roots are now strong enough to keep off the "sadfly" larva, you can make a final transition to soil composed of vegetable matter: otherwise it is advisable to stick to the secondary peat. Sufficiently strong plants on the other hand are now given a mixture of Polypodium or Osmunda fibre and Sphagnum moss, and are transplanted into larger individual pots. If coarser Osmunda is used for this, one must add a larger proportion of bog-moss than with the thick-fibred Polypodium in order to prevent over desiccation.

The soil must be used or worked only in a damp state. Consequently the cultures need not be either watered or syringed for some time, and sensitive finger-tips are required. Above all, care must be taken to provide plenty of moisture with vaporisers. Only gradually and according to individual requirement need plants be syringed, some lightly, others more strongly. The plants must, however, not be allowed to dry out completely during growth.

The time for transplanting is generally fixed by the state of growth of each orchid. It is a matter of maintaining them and aiding them by timely pricking out and transplanting. In addition growth can now be considerably accelerated through fertilisers which are readily available.

The young plants grown by the asymbiotic method which are still living without fungi must now find room as near as possible to the mother plant so that they can be readily infected by the natural root-fungus. According to the latest experiences further growth is said to succeed without a fungus but there is still a lack of scientific support and longer observation is needed.

The difficulties peculiar to the raising of *Paphiopedilums* have not yet been completely overcome. Thus for example, the symbiotic method is still unsuccessful with this species. On the other hand, the asymbiotic method can bring about not only good results but failures also.

VEGETATIVE PROPAGATION

Propagation by division does not play a large part in growing orchids, as there is not a great deal of opportunity for it. In contrast to the sexual propagation by seed, the asexual is a matter of propagation by vegetative means. That is to say, single plants can be rooted from divisions of living plants. One of the best known methods of increasing plants is by "cuttings". The next in order of importance is that of dividing plants. Many of them develop young on their stem joints and these can also be used for propagation; they can even be grown from offshoots. There are also other possibilities of this kind as, for example, the bulbils of lilies.

These various possibilities that nature makes use of and man has taken over in a practical way fall under the heading of vegetative i.e. asexual propagation.

We will now deal in greater detail with the special methods of propagating orchids.

CUTTINGS

Cuttings are now only made in exceptional cases. For example, plants of *Anoectochilus, Haemaria disolor,* and *Macodes petola* can be increased by cuttings placed in a well-shaded hot frame in shallow pots with pure Sphagnum. You can also cut long Vanilla growths into pieces with two leaf-buds each and they will likewise root quickly in pots with plenty of Sphagnum, and a little fern-root.

The cutting is divided off from the mother plant with a very sharp knife. The cut must not be made directly below the leaf bud or stipule, but some distance from it, usually on a small sideways thickening of the stem. The cut is made horizontally through the stem at about the spot where the thickening reduces down again to the normal stem, mostly under the third bud.

With valuable and sensitive cuttings such as those from the *Anoectochilus, Macodes,* etc., one must proceed with the greatest care in order to avoid losses. It is as well, therefore, to cover the severed surface of the cuttings with a thick coating of ground charcoal before putting them into damp moss. This is to prevent rot from setting in.

DIVISION

This method can be used solely with sympodial i.e. bush orchids. In particular the genus *Paphiopedilum* can be increased only by this vegetative method, much used in specialised nurseries. Division is resorted to in most cases when the plants have become too big.

To tear a plant indiscriminately into little bits is quite wrong. By doing so nearly all the roots would be broken and ruined; also excessive division so weakens the individual piece that it requires the closest attention for several years if it is to become strong and fit to bear blooms.

The individual plants should be taken out of the pot with special care so as not to damage the ball of roots, which must be carefully shaken out and washed in water in order to remove the old soil thoroughly. You then try—again taking great care—to unravel the tangle of roots and find the places where the plant will naturally come apart with the least pull.

If in spite of every care roots are damaged, cut off the broken ones a little above the break with a sharp knife. In normal cases the plant then puts out side-roots. Care must be taken when potting the divided plants to see that the healthy roots remain undamaged; this considerably speeds up the growth.

Strong specimens of *Cattleyas, Laelias, Epidendrums* etc. can also be increased by division. Plants whose roots lie near the surface of the soil can be divided with a knife prior to repotting. The advantage of this is that the divided plants get used to independance before they are isolated.

The individual pseudo-bulbs which are severed according to their age when repotting takes place, also provide an opportunity for vegetative increase. But one must make sure that the latent second eye near the base of the root is still healthy. Bulbs that do not have this prerequisite rot, because no new growth can be expected from them.

This method is most likely to succeed with the *Cymbidiums*. The pseudo-bulbs are fairly closely planted in pots or shallow pans in soil mixed with plenty of Sphagnum, and kept warmer than usual.

The bulbs that have a shoot and corresponding roots are gradually planted out in pots with the usual soil. The atmosphere is kept moist rather than the small plants themselves.

A further opportunity for vegetative increase is afforded by those orchids which grow small plants called adventitious growths on their stems, in the angle of the leaf or on the surface. Such plants appear on the stems of some species of *Epidendrums,* at the end of some *Thunia* stalks and also occasionally on bulbs in some *Dendrobiums*. They can be planted in pots with the usual soil for further growth. It is known, too, that some *Phalaenopsis* are able to grow adventitious plants from the inflorescence and on their own roots.

Asexual increase, as well as sexual, plays an important part but not all plants lend themselves to this. The advantage lies in a shortened period of cultivation; plants grown from cuttings are generally ready for sale considerably earlier than those grown from seed.

MYCORRHIZA

We have already seen that symbiotic fungi in the roots of orchids perform an important vital function. It is of further interest to know that they consist only of mycelia or threads (hence the name of thread-fungus). They pass through the substratum, surrounding the orchid with them. Professor Burgeff counts them as belonging to the *Hymenomycetan* family (hymen = skin, mycetan = fungi).

Up to the present two species of mycorrhiza are known, namely *Rhizoctonia* and *Corticium*.

The various kinds of Rhizoctonia serves as germinating aids to most of the exotic orchids. It was ascertained by a process of isolation that *Rhizoctonia repens* serves as a symbion to various kinds of *Paphiopedilum*. It has also shown itself active with

Angraecum, Brassavola, Catasetum, Cattleya, Coelogyne, and others through experimental sowings.

On the other hand, it was discovered from the roots of the genera *Anguloa* and *Lycaste* that *Rhizoctonia subilis* was a symbion, whilst according to Burgeff, *Corticium catonii* has proved to be the germinating fungus of the different species of *Cymbidium*.

In general closely related genera have one symbion in common. At the same time, the dividing line between genera of orchid and root fungus does not appear to follow strict natural laws. The symbion *Rhizoctonia repens* proves this; it can act as germinating fungus to a number of species.

It frequently happens with cultivated plants that they rid themselves of their symbiotic fungus and fungi can no longer be found in their roots.

This is one of many problems that remain to be clarified.

CHAPTER VI

ORCHIDS AS INDOOR PLANTS

Much patience and interest are needed for growing orchids indoors. Those who have already looked after indoor plants will have had some useful experiences. But that alone is insufficient There are many indispensable wrinkles we need to know and a gift for careful observation is essential. Finally, there is what is called "green-fingers". By this is meant first the ability to understand how to recognise as soon as possible changes in the wellbeing of orchids, even before they begin to develop. We should be able to tell from the plants whether they like their treatment or not; for example, whether they need less or more watering, or any other treatment essential to their welfare.

The would-be orchid grower must approach his task with an open mind and endeavour to penetrate into the secrets of the orchid world. To support him in this task there is plenty of good literature to be had and his nurslings will reward his trouble with successful growth and entrancing beauty of flower.

As conditions in our living rooms are arranged primarily for human comfort, they cannot be materially altered to suit the plants. What is provided there is a well-tempered warmth, which limits our range of choice of suitable plants, but as exotic orchids are at home in nearly every region the choice is not too difficult. Tropical orchids, which demand a high temperature with plenty of moisture in the air, are naturally out of the question. Instead, we have a whole series of beautiful well-tested representatives from the sub-tropics, the temperate zones and even some from cooler regions, whose living requirements are better suited to the conditions prevailing in living rooms.

On pages 163 to 164 there is a list of orchids suitable for indoor growing. Amateurs who keep plants on their windowsills and who would like to extend their affections to orchids are advised to grow them along with their other plants. Plants, whether of like or different kinds, grow and thrive better in company. They are said to support one another, by which is meant that they create a mutually beneficial atmosphere.

Every beginner, including the orchid grower, has to pay for his experience, but anyone who is wise knows, that he can learn from his mistakes. It is as well not to begin straight away with the best and most expensive, but to try the more modest varieties first then, having gathered some experience go on to more valuable kinds.

Far more factors have to be taken into account for tending orchids than for ordinary indoor plants.

Light Conditions

The light conditions are ideal only when the full light can bear upon the plants freely and from all sides, as happens in nature. Full light is not always to be equated with full sunshine which can be harmful for plants that like the shade and particularly so for orchids.

The windows of our living-rooms receive sunshine mostly from only one point of the compass. The side facing the interior is in comparative darkness and so gets insufficient light. That means a forced adaptation, and a turning of the leaves towards the source of light, which you can clearly see happening in quick-growing plants. When you look at them from inside the room they show only the reverse side of their leaves. This results in a reduction of their work of assimilation. It is even worse for the plants when they have to do this work from behind curtains.

Orchids should be given the best source of light to be found in the house. For example, a corner window getting its light from two directions instead of one is much more favourable; so also is a glass-covered verandah and a bay-window. Most favourable of all and closest to natural conditions is a small greenhouse adjoining the house.

But to return to the single window with which many amateurs

have to be content. It can be facing in any direction except due north. If signs of sunburn appear in particularly hot summers and southern districts of Europe, the rays of the sun should be rendered less dazzling in the hottest part of the day by translucent curtains. Danger of burning only arises in the height of summer or from a southerly aspect. On clear, sunny days protection from dazzle should be afforded from about 10.30 a.m. to 3 p.m. After that, or whenever dull weather sets in, the curtains can be drawn back. If the sky clears, the plants must be protected again. It would be injurious to them if these routine operations were not carried out in detail. The more punctilously they are done the better. Small infringements committed daily can so mount up that the flower—our greatest reward— fails in spite of all the labour and love expended on the plant.

Risk of burning by the sun's rays is much greater in a greenhouse than from behind a window, so the plants need a correspondingly longer period of shade. In autumn and even more in winter, light conditions are very unfavourable so we can replace daylight by artificial light by means of electric light tubes. This can be done before dawn or after dusk. If the plants are to feel any effect the lighting should last at least two and probably four hours every day.

WATERING

Rainwater has proved best for orchids because it is the cleanest and softest. Those who have the opportunity should collect it by means of a water-butt from the gutters of the roof and use it on the plants. Houses in towns, however, usually only have tap water which has come from under ground and may bring with it all kinds of harmful components.

Above all the water used must be as free from lime as possible. The water supply of most towns is softened and can safely be used with orchids. It has a PH 7 value and so is neutral. But in towns where this does not apply, the water is not always usable and has to be tested; one can soften it by adding sodium carbonate. In the first place tap water must be left standing long enough to enable it to get rid of harmful components. When used it should have the same temperature as the room, about 18° Centigrade. In summer, which is the main growing time of orchids, water furthers growth considerably if it is a few degrees warmer than the inside temperature.

CONCENTRATION OF HYDROGEN IONS (PH = value)

Before we concern ourselves with watering proper we must touch on a difficult point but one which is of far-reaching importance for indoor growing. It is this question of concentration of hydrogen ions, known for short as PH (*Pondus Hydrongenii* = mass of hydrogen). The would-be orchid grower must not be discouraged if he does not understand everything straight away. He can comfort himself with the thought that even when little was known about concentration of hydrogen ions, horticulture had magnificent flowers to show. Moreover, we shall limit ourselves in our descriptions to what is absolutely necessary and will simplify the complicated processes as much as possible.

A continual chemical change is going on in the soil with the help of tiny creatures and in accordance with definite laws. This liberates the so-called ions which have a fundamental influence on all plants. By far the most important are the acid hydrogen ions (chemical letter H) and the alkaline hydroxyl ions (chemical letters O H) which are juxtaposed in such a way that they neutralise each other's effect when they are present in equal quantities. In such a case the soil is described as neutral; in other cases it is either acid or alkaline. Recently way have been found to measure, exactly, the relative quantity of free hydrogen ions i.e. their concentration. The result is expressed by the numbers one to fourteen which are placed after the letter. They are to be read as powers of ten and give each time the number of litres which contain one gramme of hydrogen ions. This PH^5 (also written P H = 5) means that $10^5 = 100,000$ litres of pure water contain one gramme of free hydrogen ions. PH^3 (1 gramme to $10^3 = 1,000$ litres) would mean a one hundred fold strengthening of the concentration. PH^9 (1 gramme to $10^9 = $ a thousand million litres) would mean a ten thousand fold diluting of it.

For reasons we need not go into here, within this scale of 14, P H values and P O H values (i.e. values for the opposing concentration of hydroxyl ions) always add up to that figure. The last one quoted P H value = 9, means a P O H value of 5, a very strong calcination. And with a value P H ⁹ we have already passed the limit that plants are able to bear. It means certain death for nearly all plant life. With P H ⁷, on the other hand, there is an equalisation of acids and bases: it is the neutral point of the scale. The range of P H ⁷ to P H ¹ comprises the acids. Their strength increases with the diminishing number of P H, while P H ⁷ to P H ¹⁴ includes the range of alkaline reactions. Their strength increases with the number of P H.

This table may serve for a better understanding of the P H figures and to an easier application in practice.

P H larger than 7.5   = alkaline reaction
P H between 7.5 and 6.5 = neutral reaction
P H   ,,   6.4 ,, 4.6 = weak acid reaction
P H   ,,   4.4 ,, 4   = acid reaction
P H less than 4   = strong acid reaction

It is obvious that the kinds of soil in which the plants have to find their nourishment is not a matter of indifference to them. In fact every species requires for good growth the P H value which suits it. One prospers best in alkaline soil, another in acid, yet others want a neutral soil. In the natural state all this happens of itself. Plants settle in the places that suit them and the rainwater, which is almost pure chemically, and in any case has no harmful components in it, keeps in check the salts contained in the moisture in the ground which might possibly change the P H value. It often does this by washing a part of them away, especially the alkaline salt, calcium, which would otherwise quickly lead to calcination, if present in too great a concentration.

It is much more difficult for our indoor plants. Continual evaporation increases the content of harmful salts and with tapwater which may contain lime we go on adding to them. Our orchids, however, prefer to grow in a slightly acid soil P H value about 5. Too low a pH value hinders germination, too high a one forces it. So it is advisable to buy litmus paper and make frequent checks. If it turns orange or orange-yellow it indicates the right pH value. This paper serves also to test the solution of the medium on which we are sowing as well as in the water used for watering. Further one ought only to use rain-water, because tap-water, sooner or later, brings about the dreaded calcination. At least one should let it stand a few hours and test its H value from time to time. Means have recently become available for improving it.

Do not worry too much about maintaining the pH value. Sowings of orchids do indeed require exact observance of the rules, but grown plants flourish quite well in a neutral concentration. Moreover, the vegetable matter in Sphagnum and fern-roots corresponds exactly to the desired pH value, as has been mentioned elsewhere. If their vigorous growth should flag, however, it would be as well in each case to test the water used.

Correct Watering

This is the most difficult thing in tending orchids: many plants have fallen victims to inexpert watering. There are no general rules; it is more a matter of close observation and feeling. The novice must first get to know what a dry root-ball looks like on the surface in order to be sure of picking out the dry plants if possible at first sight. For it should be only the dry plants that are singled out and watered.

As a matter of principle, watering must take place in the early forenoon, so that by evening any superfluous water has drained out of the pots and no stagnant moisture remains at night. This careful method of watering with small doses applies particularly to the dark autumn and winter months during which plant activity comes almost to a standstill.

One need not be so careful about watering in the summer when orchids are at their growing peak and their need of moisture is greatest. They should have plenty of it. Individual plants, therefore, can be thoroughly watered about twice a week according to their degree of dryness. Later on, when the heat is diminishing, they can mostly manage with one watering a week. Great heat from the sun, and the dry air it produces, causes quicker evaporation in the plants than in cool months and dull light.

We need to keep a special eye on those orchids which demand an annual period of rest. In doing so we must distinguish those with pseudo-bulbs, which shed all their leaves, from those which retain them throughout.

The former, which usually have thick bulbs with water stored in them, are kept completely dry e.g. *Anguloa, Catasetum, Lycaste* etc., Only when the new growth appears and a few roots have sprouted, should a start be made with moderate quantities of water. The other group, whose bulbs retain their stem and leaves, must be given smaller quantities of water from time to time so that their bulbs do not shrivel e.g. *Cattleyas, Laelias,* etc., Only the orchids without any bulbs have no period of rest. They are kept damper because of their greater need of moisture.

HUMIDITY

In windy weather and the hot sun we notice that the orchids have suddenly increased their thirst. Their need of water rises and we have to take the watering-can to them more frequently This need of moisture is caused by evaporation from the leaves, accelerated by increasing heat and slowing down as the heat decreases.

The variations in the rate of the evaporation which is constantly drawing off water from the almost 95% content of the plants, are determined by the moisture in the atmosphere, according to how rich this is in the air surrounding the plants in their natural state.

This so-called relative humidity is in close relationship to the temperature of the air. Humidity decreases as the temperature rises and vice-versa.

The degree of humidity varies in different zones. In the tropics it is almost 100%, in the sub-tropics about 80%. But the moisture content of the air often changes considerably from region to region within these zones when special circumstances, such as steady air currents, deserts, marshland or lakes exercise an influence on it.

In nature the loss of water through evaporation is replaced by dew and rain. But we have to regulate by our own efforts the appropriate degree of humidity in the atmosphere around the plants as well as the watering of them, because they are not affected by the rains. In greenhouses you can use water from a hosepipe as much as you like to achieve the required humidity, the plants and their surroundings can be sprinkled several times a day: but in our living rooms we have to consider the furniture.

So we shall confine ourselves to a selection of those orchids which need only a humidity roughly comparable to that of our own climate. In the warm season, especially if it is very hot, frequent daily syringing cannot be avoided but this is bearable in a living room. As an alternative, wide shallow bowls of water can be put on the window sill and they will increase humidity. The orchid plants placed on up-turned flower-pots in the bowls then stand in the sphere of evaporation.

In winter a receptacle filled with water can be placed or hung above the stove or other source of warmth, especially when the heating has to be full on.

FRESH AIR

Fresh air is just as necessary to plants as to human beings. But whether the window should be opened or not depends on the weather. There is hardly anything against opening it in the warm season of the year and it is part of good culture. A draught, however, spells death to the plants; to avoid it, only the upper ventilators of the window should be opened and where none exists, it would be well worth while putting one in. In spring and autumn they should be opened only on mild days and for short spells at a time. Cold and frosty air must be kept from the orchids just as much as a draught.

In conservatories the arrangements for ventilation also serve to balance the temperatures in the various sections and at the same time to protect the plants from being scorched by the strong action of the sun's rays. Sun shining through the glass-roofs gives a much stronger heat than through the windows of our living rooms.

TEMPERATURES

Exotic orchids have very varying needs for warmth, which change according to the situation of their natural habitat. But even their needs are not rigidly fixed; there is a certain amount of play one way or the other, which enables us to divide them with few exceptions, into three groups each having a different requirement in the matter of warmth.

Members of the First Group demand an average winter temperature of 18-22 degrees Centigrade in daytime, consequently they are called *warm house orchids*.

Members of the Second Group require an average day temperature of 16-18 degrees Centigrade and are referred to as *temperate-house orchids*.

Members of the Third Group for which an average temperature of 8-12 degrees Centigrade is sufficient are called *cool house orchids*.

Specialised nurseries wanting to grow all three groups must possess greenhouses, each with the appropriate temperature. Only groups two and three can be considered for growing in rooms behind a single window, unless there is a closed glass case in the room, in which the high moisture content of the air required by hothouse orchids, can be attained. It would be best to consult an expert about setting up such a glass case or making any other arrangement.

In a hot summer you can manage without additional heating for group two, but when there is a long spell of cool weather, enough to make us feel cold in a room, then greenhouse orchids must be given additional heat. The plants make their maximum growth in summer; at that time they are completing the year's growth, of stem, leaves and construction of the flower buds. If very cool weather upsets this steady growth, development stops and this always has an unfavourable effect on the formation of the buds. The plants then either have deformed flowers or none at all. Such drops in temperature must, therefore, always be met with a compensating amount of heat.

At night the temperature should be lowered by about 4-5 degrees Centigrade in all indoor growing places. This reproduces the conditions of nature where for the most part nights are cooler. Also the plants take a rest from growth at night. For example the intake of carbonic acid, which acts only in sunlight, halts at night. The drooping of the leaves on many plants is a sure indication of it.

In the winter, too, both day and night temperature must be lowered by 4-5 degrees as a general rule. At this time the whole organism of the plant gradually comes to a standstill, conditioned by the strong reduction in the warmth and light of the sun.

It is undesirable that orchids should put out shoots in winter, because they will have developed in insufficient light and will lack strength. Unfortunately this can easily happen when a room becomes so overheated that the temperature prescribed for the winter is not adhered to.

COMPOSTS AND THEIR PREPARATION

The search for suitable compost matter, especially for the unusual tree-loving orchids, has long exercised the minds of growers. It took a good time before the present well-tried material was discovered.

As the roots of the epiphytic orchids are more exposed and better adapted to air than to soil, a looser material letting in more air had to be found to correspond to the need of the roots for air. At the same time it had to be capable of resisting too rapid a decomposition.

The roots of certain ferns fulfil these requirements. The roots of *Polypodium vulgare* (known as the speckled fern), thorn fern, (*Aspidium spinnulosum*) and royal fern (*Osmunda regalis*) are used. This last is now the most important because of its durability.

All three ferns are to be found in European woods. Of these *Polypodium* and *Aspidium* are grown in Europe for this purpose and appear commercially as *Polypodium* or *Aspidium* fibre, whereas the royal fern *Osmunda* fibre has to be imported from North America, Italy and Japan, as it does not grow in sufficient quantities in the other countries of Europe. *Osmunda* fibre is ideal for growing orchids because of its durability and coarse consistency. Neither of the other fibres can equal it.

In addition bog-mosses (kinds of sphagnum) are used and are found on high moorlands. Three kinds are mentioned in orchid literature. *Sphagnum acutifolium, Sphagnum cymbifolium* and *Sphagnum squarrosum*: the last named is a large-headed kind. It is much more productive and long-lasting than the other two, which should only be resorted to in case of dire need; it is sold as dried sphagnum, which is, however, mostly dead. It is better to use living sphagnum, especially when one covers the surfaces of the orchid pot carefully with heads of moss, as used always to be done. The old orchid growers followed the maxim: "If the moss grows, the orchid grows." By that they meant that the growth of the moss on top of the pot was an indication that things outside and inside the pot were healthy and suited to the requirements of the orchid. But the sphagnum can be kept alive only by treating it with rain-water. Dried beech leaves, too, are used as compost matter, particularly with the *Cattleyas,* though more for eking out purposes and cheapness. For terrestrial orchids leaf mould, garden soil, and river sand can be used. The small quantities of the right composition needed by most amateurs can best be obtained from orchid nurseries ready for use.

MIXING OF COMPOSTS

The various fern fibres and sphagnum are used only in a clean state and chopped small. The roots should be thoroughly washed in water before they are chopped up. If the sphagnum has been gathered in its natural state it must lie in water for a time or be treated with slugicide to get rid of the snails and chopped into equal sized pieces. After being washed the *Polypodium, Aspidium* and *Osmunda* fibres are chopped into pieces about the size of a walnut.

It is important to remove the woody stems of the ferns, for once cut and wet, they tend to rot and the fungi that develop may destroy the roots of the whole plant.

The compost should be mixed as follows:

For orchids that grow on trees and have stronger roots it is best to use sphagnum mixed with osmunda fibre because its coarseness suits the tougher roots. For smaller orchids with finer roots add to the osmunda fibre a portion of polypodium or aspidium fibre and a corresponding portion of sphagnum in order to ensure a compact compost. The coarse aerated compost naturally dries more quickly than the denser kind. That is why the thin delicate roots of small orchids would more easily come to harm through drought in the coarse material.

When planting, therefore, we must always start with the consideration that the more tender the roots the closer and moister must be the compost, and the more robust the roots the coarser and more airy the material should be. These mixtures can be changed at will according to the strength of the roots. In doing so one must take into consideration the fact that the sphagnum is able to absorb many times its own weight of water.

The more moss we use the longer will water from the can remain in the pot. Too much water, however, can lead to stagnant and unhealthy conditions, because the moss and polypodium fibre, more quickly decompose than under normal circumstances. Acids are formed by this decomposition and they attack the roots. In practice this is called souring the orchid. Such a souring of the compost necessitates repotting in fresh compost if the plant is to be saved. If the season is unfavourable for this additional repotting, one should go about it very carefully. In any case it means a disturbance of the orchid's growth from which it will recover gradually.

Expirienced growers recognise the particular needs of their individual plants and make the mixture to suit them. Such knowledge for amateurs is gained through considerable effort and experience.

If the compost is to consist of two components only, take two of osmunda fibre to one of sphagnum. With three components all three, osmunda and polypodium fibre and moss, should be in equal proportions. In many cases the proportion of moss will appear too large but it can be reduced at will, and the same applies to the other two components.

For the terrestrial orchids, in most cases one should keep to the same basic mixture as for the epiphytic ones adding soil as the need arises. One must take into account the fact that these orchids perhaps grow in soil, but also in many cases in a loose humus, that is, in a well aerated soil. Even for many species that do not live in wooded areas. e.g. the *Paphiopedilum,* it has been proved that a loose, porous material is preferable.

The following scheme makes a serviceable mixture for terrestrial orchids:

1 part osmunda fibre, 1 part polypodium fibre, $\frac{1}{2}$ part moss and $\frac{1}{2}$ part fibrous loam or soil.

With its pH value, which varies between pH 5 and pH 6, such a mixture corresponds roughly to the normal needs.

The condition of the habitat of tropical or sub-tropical terrestrial orchids are not always easy to imitate and reproduce in our latitudes. The chemical content of the soils is quite different. For example, if a certain plant grows in loam, this loam may be very far from resembling the loam in our part of the world.

The best known in the tropics is red laterite loam, which is formed from the weathering of certain crystalline rocks and is not found at all in Europe. And if you do use loam, it must be the infertile kind which is found well below the soil. If there is no old sandstone loam available it is better to make do with a good turf soil or even with normal soil. The quantity of the particular kind of soil added to the compost for terrestrial orchids must not be so large that its density entirely destroys the loose and porous character of the compost itself. Here, too, it is a matter of experience and sensitivity as to whether you always get the proportion right or not.

GROWING IN POTS

The ordinary flower pots have proved excellent, even for the tree loving varieties. These latter grow more naturally on cork bark, acacia boughs or on lumps of fern, all of which can be used with success, and lend themselves to the possibility of hanging the plants up.

If old pots are used they must, of course, be thoroughly washed inside and out and left to dry. If new pots are used follow the usual practice and leave them under water until no more air bubbles rise. If this is not done, the roots fasten so firmly on to the side of the pot that they all break, when transplanting, and cannot be freed in any other way than by tearing them off. This means a great loss of roots which is almost irreparable. The pots must be dry; they should not be used while wet.

For the larger specimens of epiphytic orchids which usually decorate conservatories use, for preference, square wooden baskets made of square strips . The most durable ones are of oak or acacia wood and the orchid grower makes them himself.

Always collect the sherds from broken flower pots in order to have a sufficient supply on hand when transplanting. They play an important part because the pots used for epiphytic orchids are half-filled with well-washed sherds placed as nearly upright as possible. Before that, the hole at the bottom must be closed with a sherd so that no insect can crawl in and eat the roots.

This measure allows for the speedy draining of the compost and drying off the root-ball, thus contributing to the health of the plant.

REPOTTING

Repotting or transplanting becomes necessary when the plants are so strong that there is no more room in the pot for the next year's growth, or when the growing material needs renewing. It is one of the most important operations and demands skill and understanding Where opportunity allows, one should learn from an expert; as with everything else it is a matter of practice and experience.

Repotting must, of course, be done at the proper time. In specialist undertakings it is usually done within a two or three year cycle. The different kinds and species which flower in autumn or winter are transplanted in the spring after the new shoots appear. Before the work is started, the young growths must already be showing root-tips. It is good, too, to pot during warm, sunny periods, for the orchids like a higher temperature after being potted up and give better growth with extra warmth.

Orchids that flower in the spring or a bit later, are transplanted as soon as they have finished flowering. As this is nearly always accompanied by some loss of roots, the plants suffer a good deal in their growth. Increased warmth from the sun is the best thing to overcome this. There should be no watering for several weeks after transplanting, instead, the plants should be sprinkled two or three times a day with slightly warmed rain water. That is the quickest way to get them over the shock of repotting.

The compost must be damp but not wet when used. Orchids which shed their leaves in their non-growing period thereafter lose their roots and only need watering when the new ones have taken full hold of the compost. Exactly the same procedure is adopted with bulbless and evergreen species (e.g. *Paphiopedilum*) after they have been transplanted. But the conditions of their environment, such as higher temperature and greater humidity which have to be produced by spraying the plants, paths and walls, are better created in the greenhouse than in the sitting room.

In the year in which the orchids have been transplanted do not expect many, if any, flowers at all, as the orchids need all their strength to restore full root action. All withered parts, such as old shrivelled bulbs, dried and rotting roots, and sheaths must be examined to see if they shield scale or mealy bugs. This is a good opportunity for destroying these pests.

Sometimes the lice lodge so deeply in the crutch between roots and stems that we can only get at them with a toothbrush or rags soaked in warm soapy water. The back bulbs which are suitable for propagation are collected and treated in the way described in the section on propagation by division.

When the plant has been taken out of the pot, which often has to be smashed on account of the roots sticking too fast, the old material is removed with as little harm as possible to the roots, which later on are washed out. The broken roots are cut off with a sharp knife just above the damaged section.

For plants with a biennial cycle, particularly *Cattleyas* and *Laelias* the new pots, must be of sufficient size to allow room for at least two years' growth. That applies of course only to strong and healthy plants which are pretty sure to flower. Otherwise the pots should not be too large.

First the hole at the bottom is covered with a sherd and then the pot is filled with sherds to a third or a half according to the size of the rootstock. On top of the sherds put a thin layer of compost. The roots are set in this and surrounded with more of the compost. With a blunt dibber press the compound firmly so that all holes are filled in and the plant gets a firm root hold. The pot is then filled up leaving a margin for watering of about one and a half centimetres.

With sympodial orchids care must further be taken that their rootstock lies firmly on the compost.

With the monopodials the dead lower part of the stem should be cut off from the healthy part before transplanting. Orchids belonging to this group, having one stem, e.g. *Angraecum, Phalaeonopsis, Vanda,* etc., are always planted in the middle of the pot, whereas those of the sympodial group are set with their bulb at the edge of the pot on account of their creeping rhizome; the new shoots find room in the pot and not down the side.

Terrestrial orchids are transplanted in the same way, but using the compost prescribed for terrestrial orchids.

Only epiphytic orchids are put into wooden baskets or on cork bark or branches of trees. This method of planting fits in with their natural habitat. As each plant needs to be hung up, only a few can be accommodated on the side walls of a window in a room.

The nature of many orchid flowers makes it necessary to

plant in wooden baskets because of their pendent flower spikes. Small orchids such as the genus *Oncidium* like growing on cork or lumps of wood and look more natural there.

Transplanting into wooden baskets proceeds in the same way as transplanting into pots, but we can leave out the deep layer of sherds which assures aeration and drainage because the compost in the basket is exposed on all sides to the air and this ensures rapid drying out.

Orchids which push their flowers down through the compost, as is the case with the genus *Stanhopean*, are not given an underlayer of sherds at all. Only where the flowers hang down over the side of the basket put a thin layer of sherds over the bottom and over that spread the appropriate compost. The plant is put into it and pressed in firmly from all sides with more compost, just as with pots; do let it overarch the top of the basket a little and do not bother about leaving a margin for watering.

The size of the basket should be chosen very carefully and be too large rather than too small, any airy space for hanging the basket can be used e.g. by putting hooks in the beams of the ceiling.

Acacia boughs and cork bark are sawn into sizes to suit the plant and the normal compost with *polypodium* fibre for tree-growing orchids is used. The plants are firmly fixed in their natural position by means of copper wire and in order not to damage them moss is pushed under the places where the wire bites. Practical experience shows that the roots grow along the crevices in the bark where moisture remains longest and that they like a thinner substratum.

Plants set up in this way cannot be kept damp enough with a watering-can or by syringing. They are dipped carefully in a pail of water in such a way as not to wet and harm the young shoots, buds and flowers.

Hanging plants dry much more quickly than potted ones and need constant attention. At the height of summer individual plants might have to be dipped every day if the circumstances require it.

MANURING

Manuring has always been looked upon as a great problem and thoughtless use of commercial manures has brought about many regrettable losses. Strong, imported terrestrial orchids can be successfully manured, as indeed can all plants if one goes about it sensibly. But with the epiphytes manuring is a real problem and beginners should be strictly warned against the use of commercial or artificial manures.

The private grower succeeds best with organic manures (humus). Dry or liquid cow-dung has long proved its worth and horn-shavings and bone-meal are also good. Cow-dung and horn-shavings contain principally nitrogen, and bone-meal contains phosphorus.

Liquid cow-dung, of course, is out of the question for indoor growing on account of its unpleasant smell, but it can be added to the compost mixture in its dry form and in small doses. Horn-meal should not be used; it is too concentrated.

Dry cow-dung consists of pure cow droppings dried in the open air. It is then broken up with a hammer, rubbed through a sieve with a medium mesh and mixed with the compost in the proportion of 20 grammes to a litre of water. To this is added a solution of about 10 to 12 grammes of bone-meal to the litre.

Such doses of manure can hardly do any harm, even to epiphytes. The manure is mild in character and it gradually dissolves in the plant mixture. In actual practice the quantity is decided in each case by experience.

Cow-dung as a well-tried manure for greenhouse orchids must be well decomposed. Liquid dung is only administered when orchids are urgently in need of it, notably in the summer months when growth is at its maximum, but even then it should be administered only once a week. The dung must be watered down till it is straw-coloured. Manuring takes places on days when the sky is overcast or in the evening after sunset, otherwise scorching of the leaves may occur. For the same reason pots should never be watered with liquid manure when dry but only when they are moist all through.

At the end of the summer, when the growth for that year is fairly well formed, slacken off the watering till it happens only once a fortnight. When growth ceases completely, there should be no more watering. The pseudo-bulbs and the leaves are now approaching maturity i.e. they are approaching their winter rest.

More recently the use of organic toxins has been recommended and they have a stimulating effect. This provokes in the plant an increased assimilation which results in advancing the growth.

Before the World War I Professor Dr. Rudolf Lieske developed his orchid fertiliser "Orchidal" which has been recognised by all contemporary experts as standard. Unfortunately, he died too soon. "Orchidal" was the result of many years' experiment made with the purpose of finding a product based specially on the particular needs of orchids in the matter of nourishment. He discovered this in lignite which, combined with various elements, forms the basis of the preparation. How to procure this lignite after the World War II gave Lieske great concern. The only suitable kind came from Niederlausitz, the other side of the iron-curtain. Unfortunately, death put an end to his endeavours in 1950, and with his death hopes of resuming the manufacture of 'Orchidal' have disappeared for the time being.

The German Orchid Society's publication, *The Orchid,* has recommended amateurs to use a fertiliser called "Oak Beer", discovered in America. To make it you need a wide-necked vessel, a handful of dried oak leaves and a jug or can. Pour a couple of litres of water into the receptacle and add 15 to 20 leaves that have been rubbed to a powder in the hands, so as to remove the strong central nerves. Stir until all the leaf particles are thoroughly soaked and then stir at repeated intervals for three days. The solution, which has a brownish beer colour, is ready after the three days and is filtered into a three litre can containing one litre of water.

The solution is given to the plants two or three times a month, during their period of maximum growth. According to Bohlmann, the same effect should be obtained with small green beech twigs hung a number of times in water, but only for a short time at a stretch.

PESTS AND HOW TO COMBAT THEM

Orchids not only have friends but, unfortunately, foes as well and it is a question of driving them off before they do any irreparable harm. As a general rule the number which may be found in a greenhouse is fairly large. They have mostly been brought in with the plants imported from abroad; however, since importation has considerably slackened off, this nuisance has decreased. We need to pay the greatest attention and notice changes in health and even the slightest signs of damage, so that we can intervene as quickly as possible.

Animal pests may put in an appearance in spite of the greatest care, but fungus pests are mostly due to mistakes in cultivation. These happen when, for example, warmth and humidity have not been sufficiently well balanced.

Prevention is the best method of combatting these pests. This is done by either spraying, whether there are any pests or not, with pure nicotine or fumigating at regular intervals. Both methods apply only to greenhouse cultivation on a large scale and in the use of cyanide gas legal provisions have to be observed. Only harmless preventatives should be used with indoor plants and here it is more a matter of individual plants which can be dealt with by a sprayer.

Cleanliness is the best defence. It is the supreme rule for greenhouses, that the noxious creatures should be given no hide-outs in dirt at the corners or under the staging.

The common field-snail (*Agriolimax agrestis*) which comes out at night is a much dreaded foe. Its eggs and the creature itself get on to the plants and into the culture through the moss. They are all the more dangerous because they carry on their depredations during the night and sleep during the day in holes and corners. We often find the flower stems eaten and they also work their mischief on the tender leaves of the young plants.

The flower stalks can be protected with small bands of cotton wool. Snails can only eat the tenderest parts towards the top of the stalk. So the lump of cotton wool should be placed well down where the stalk is quite tough. The snails can only get over this barrier if the wool has been made wet with spraying. So during this period spraying is not done, but if it should happen by mistake, the wool should be replaced.

Of course this measure does not destroy the pest. Over and above laying down slug-killer and half a potato hollowed out, the grower would do well to pay frequent visits in the dark with a torch. This should be done with all the more vigour when the characteristic tracks of shiny slime the snails leave behind have been noticed in the daytime. Slug-killer is an effective means of dealing with them.

Hollowed-out potatoes are put out late in the afternoon. They serve as traps not only for the snails but also for other orchid pests such as wood lice *(Onicus asellus)* blackbeetles *(Periplaneta americana)* and their relative the cockroach *(Blatta orientalis)*. They are all root pests and like the tender tips of the roots best. The most effective way of dealing with these pests is by repeatedly powdering all the surroundings with an insect-killer.

The various greenfly (Aphis) which, especially when they appear in large numbers, harm the leaves can quickly be got rid of by syringing with an insecticide.

There is as yet no certain preventive against the shield-scale *(Crysomphalus)* that does not, at the same time, harm the plant. The most useful is the old method of washing the leaves with a toothbrush dipped in soapy water. The same applies to the mealy bug or cochineal *(Coccinia)* which are protected by a woolly covering of wax. Like the greenfly and scale they suck away all the green parts of the plant, especially the underside of the leaves, whilst the upper side, through perforation, becomes spotted with yellow, at first imperceptibly, but eventually the leaves die off too soon. The yellow orchid-thrips and the tiny spider mite, known as the red-spider, do the same.

Pure nicotine is the only effective means against the black-fly and the red-spider. The liquid is used in a diluted form of 20 cubic centimetres to ten litres of water. Sprayings should be repeated at short intervals until no creatures are left. Window-sill orchids, however, are best washed in warm soapy water if they have any of these pests. Pure nicotine is not pleasant in the house.

It has already been pointed out that the appearance of fungus pests is caused in most cases by faulty treatment. An example would be the spotted leaf disease in the gens *Phalaenopsis* which regularly appears as black rot on the leaves, if the plants have been kept too cold or damp in autumn and winter. It does not appear if the plants have been given the steady temperature of 22° Centigrade needed for their well being.

Badly decaying plants should be isolated as far as possible from healthy ones and treated with a solution of corrosive Upsulun or Ceresan which can be obtained from the chemist. The plants are sprayed once or more, or dipped in the prescribed solution, according to the degree of contamination. The plants can sometimes be saved by these means if they are kept dry in open air afterwards.

The signs of damage from a fungus attack are not widely different from those caused by bacteria or fission-fungus *(Schizomycetes)*. *Bacterium oncidii,* for example, produces on the leaves of the oncidium the bright yellow, oily spots which spread fairly quickly. Similar brown spots which ultimately rot are caused on the leaves of varieties of *Paphiopedilum* by *Bacterium cypripedii*. To counter this, Nicolai recommends spraying with a 2% solution of copper sulphate. A 25% solution of Germisan is also said to have the same effect.

Great attention must be paid to the presence of ants. Above all they nurse and feed greenfly and scale and carry them on to the plant. The ants regard them as a kind of milch cow. Greenfly are able to exude a sweet sticky shiny stuff called honey dew. The ants regard this as their favourite food and it is extremely interesting to watch them on the greenfly's back stroking the rear part of its body with feelers and feet in order to wheedle the drops of honey dew out of them.

Honey dew, with the addition of black mildew, produces the black coating over the leaves which not only upsets their breathing but may even ruin them completely.

Effective preparations for combatting ants can be purchased.

PFITZER'S ORCHID CLASSIFICATION

First Sub-Family - *Diandrae*

Group 1   *Cypripedilinae*

Second Sub-Family - *Monandrae*
Section 1 *Basitonae*

Group 2   *Habenarinae*   Group 4   *Disperidinae*
Group 3   *Disaeinae*

Section II *Aerotonae*
Sub-section 1 *Polychondrae*

Group	5	*Pterostylidinae*	Group	15	*Vanillinae*
,,	6	*Diuridinae*	,,	16	*Sobraliinae*
,,	7	*Thelymitrinae*	,,	17	*Cephalantherinae*
,,	8	*Prasophyllinae*	,,	18	*Gastrodiinae*
,,	9	*Drakaeinae*	,,	19	*Bletillinae*
,,	10	*Caladenuunae*	,,	20	*Cranichidinae*
,,	11	*Acianthinae*	,,	21	*Spiranthinae*
,,	12	*Cryptostylidinae*	,,	22	*Physurinae*
,,	13	*Cloraeinae*	,,	23	*Tropidiinae*
,,	14	*Listerinae*			

Sub-section II *Kerosphaereae*
Series A *Acranthae*

Group	24	*Collabiinae*	Group	30	*Laeliinae*
,,	25	*Adrorrhizinae*	,,	31	*Liparidinae*
,,	26	*Pleurothallidinae*	,,	32	*Dendrobiinae*
,,	27	*Pondeinae*	,,	33	*Glomerinae*
,,	28	*Coelogyninae*	,,	34	*Podochilinae*
,,	29	*Thuniiae*	,,	35	*Polystachyinae*

Series B. *Pleuranthae*
Sub-series 1 *Sympodiales*

Group	36	*Coraliorrhizinae*	Group	40	*Ridleyellinae*
,,	37	*Phajinae*	,,	41	*Thelasinae*
,,	38	*Bulbophyllinae*	,,	42	*Cyrtopodiinae*
,,	39	*Genyorchidinae*	,,	43	*Cymbidiinae*

Group 44 *Grobyinae*	Group 53 *Trichocentrinae*
,, 45 *Thecostelinae*	,, 54 *Comparettiinae*
,, 46 *Catasetinae*	,, 55 *Jonopsidinae*
,, 47 *Gongorinae*	,, 56 *Notyliinae*
,, 48 *Lycastinae*	,, 57 *Aspasiinae*
,, 49 *Zygopetalinae*	,, 58 *Oncidiinae*
,, 50 *Huntleyinae*	,, 59 *Ornithocephalinae*
,, 51 *Maxillarinae*	,, 60 *Telipogoninae*
,, 52 *Eulophidiinae*	,, 61 *Lockhartiinae*

Sub-series II Monopodiales

Group 62 *Dichaeinae*	Group 64 *Pterostemmatinae*
,, 63 *Pachyphyllinae*	,, 65 *Sarcanthinae*

Notes on the Orchid Classification

As an introduction to an understanding of the classification, it might be helpful to pick out the main distinguishing features of the sub-family, sections and series.

In the following explanatory notes it is not possible to take into account the different genera and species. These will be described in the next part in connection with the plates.

First Sub-Family. *Diandrae*

Professor Pfitzer had originally described the first family in his system as *Diandrae* but later he changed the name to *Pleonandrae* (meaning many males) after it had been established that the different kinds of the genera *Apostasia* and *Neuwidia* have not two stamens but three, like the *Liliaecae*.

This fact caused the famous orchid specialist, Schlechter, to take both species away from the *Orchidaceae* family and make a new family with them called the *Apostasiaceae*. By so doing he made Pfitzer's original idea once more valid, so that the term *diandrae* still holds for the first sub-division of the family.

Group 1 *Cypripedilinae*

Through Schlechter's move, this group really only embraces diandrous species which are regularly and clearly characterised by their shoe shaped lip and their kidney shaped column disc (staminode). The latter has developed from the third sterile stamen. The *Cypripedilinae* group contains only four species whose ovary is either incomplete with only one compartment or complete with three.

Second Sub-Family *Monandrae*

All orchids with only one stamen belong to this sub-family. Only the fertile stamen in their outer circle (Diagram C) opposite the middle sepal is fully formed. The two in the inner circle are sometimes identifiable in the form of staminodes. Here we find, in many sub-divisions, the great host of remaining orchids, arranged according to their salient features.

Section 1. *Basitonae.*

All the orchids of this section are distinguished by their anthers having grown firmly on to the broad base of the column which is mainly very short. Consequently there is no filament and the anther is also not sub-divided, as it is with the Acrotonae.

Terrestrial herbaceous orchids with small root tubers or fleshy spindle shaped roots, from which every year new growth is formed and dies after fructescence, are the only ones that belong to this group.

It is the same process as with our indigenous orchids which belong here.

Section 2. *Acrotonae.*

The anther in the representatives of this section does not grow on to the column as in the *Basitonae* but is joined to the bottom of the back and hangs down by a thin stalk into a cavity at the top of the column. It may also happen that it is held in an erect position by the perpendicular rostellum. All the same, the acrotonic position is easily recognisable because the adhesive disc is opposite the point of attachment.

Sub-section 1. *Polychondrae*

In this sub-section we find the acrotonic orchids, whose pollen consists of grains which are easily detachable.

Subsection II. Kerosphaerae

In contrast to the polychondrae the plants of this subsection are distinguished by sticky wax like pollinia that may sometimes be almost horn shaped.

Series A. *Acranthae*

This series is mostly characterised by terminal flower stems i.e. the stem ends in the flower or fruit.

The genus *Dendrobium* and a few unimportant ones whose flowers are arranged at the side form an exception to this rule.

Series B. *Pleuranthae*

The Pleuranthe differ from the Acranthae in that their flowers always grow out sideways from the axil of the leaf.

Sub-section 1. *Sympodiales*

This sub-section is distinguished by sympodial (many footed) formation of shoots which shows a rhizome-like (i.e. a connected) articulation.

Subsection 2. *Monopodiales*

In contra-distinction to the Sympodiales we find in this subsection only bulbless genera with a monopodial (one-footed) stem whose growing axis has unlimited growth but the lower end of the stem gradually dies off. This process is comparable to the gradual death of the pseudo bulbs of the *Sympodiales*.

A natural system of plants, of which the orchids form one, does not submit to hard and fast rules. Everywhere you come across deviations, one sort running into the other, thus making separation into different kinds, species and groups very difficult. The Greek philosophers' principle that everything is in flux applies here too, and most particularly for the botanist. Fresh knowledge may at any time bring about changes in the system.

PART II

COLOUR PLATES WITH DESCRIPTIONS

Group 1: *Cypripedilinae*

Paphiopedilum Pftz. Lady's Slipper

(syn. *Cypripedium* L.)

(Paphio = Venus, Lady; pedilon = shoe, slipper)

The name Lady's Slipper, from the shoe-shaped lip, is now in common use for *Paphiopedilum* which is one of the best known orchids. This genus is one of the most resistant, the plants remain in flower for weeks and are also long-lasting as cut flowers.

With the three related genera, *Selenipedilum, Cypripedilum* and *Phragmopedilum*, it forms the first sub-family of *Diandrae,* characterised by having only two stamens; all have the shoe-like lip.

All four genera, of which *Paphiopedilum* is the most important, can easily be distinguished by well-marked characteristics; thus *Selenipedilum* differs from *Paphiopedilum* by the one-celled ovary, whilst *Cypripedilum,* which lives in temperate regions, dies down in winter. Finally, in the species of *Phragmopedilum* the edge of the opening of the lip is always involuted; the genus *Paphioledilum* is the only one with a three-celled ovary. *Phragmopedilum* is the only genus occurring in tropical America.

Habitat: there are about 50 species of *Paphiopedilum,* which are bulbless, terrestrial plants, distributed from India across Malaya and the Moluccas to the Philippines and New Guinea, and northwards to China. Plates 1 to 6

Group: 3 *Disaeinae*

The term "uniflora" is not descriptive of the species because it has, not one, but up to five flowers, but since it is the older name it has priority in accordance with the Rules of Nomenclature.

The genus *Disa,* which contains some 120 species, is characterised by the large, helmet-shaped central sepal, the smaller petals generally behind and the always small, tongue-shaped lip which is sometimes lobed. Most of the species occur throughout Africa; a few only come from Madagascar and the Bourbon Islands, where they are terrestrial. Plate 7

Group 30: *Laeliinae*

Epidendrum L.

(epi = upon; dendron = tree, since it is an epiphyte)

As the name implies, all the representatives of this genus grow on trees. In 1927 Schlechter recognised some 750 species and the number has increased considerably since then. Almost all occur in Tropical America, a few only in the West Indies. The abundance of species indicates the variety of form within the genus. General characteristics are the labellum united with the column for a considerable distance and a strongly developed clinandrium. The range of variability of the individual organs is large. The flowers are usually medium sized, but often inconspicuously small; when they are more numerous, they are held in racemes or panicles of varying length. Many of the species are suitable for indoor cultivation.   Plates 8 to 10

Group 26: *Pleurothallidinae*

Masdevallia RUIZ ET PAV.

(Named after the Spanish Dr. Jos. Masdevall)

Masdevallia is one of the genera characterised by the triangular form of the flowers. The three sepals dominate the flower and the three-angled form is further emphasised by their tips, often prolonged into slender threads. The other organs, petals and labellum, are very short and inconspicuous. The sepals are often covered with hairs or papillae. *Masdevallias* are charming little orchids, of tufted habit, with a tendency to grotesque floral forms. The leaves are solitary on short, stunted pseudo-bulbs. The flower stalk arises from the axil of the leaf and may be erect though in many species it hangs downwards. In most cases the inflorescence bears one flower only but in some species there may be as many as eight.

The genus is of interest to all orchid growers since it only needs cool moist air for its successful growth and therefore needs cool house treatment. There are more than 150 species in the cool moist mountains of tropical Central and South America, mostly epiphytic, a few growing on rocks.   Plates 11, 12

Group 28: *Coelogyninae*

Coelogyne LDL.

(coilos = hollow; gyne = female)

The chief characteristic of this genus is the footless and usually very slender column which has no appendage. The pseudo-bulbs are never jointed. The genus belongs to the sympodial orchids and, as such, to the *Acranthae,*with terminal flowers. There are about 120 species known, many being mountain dwellers.

Plates 13, 14

Group 30: *Laeliinae*

Barkeria KN. ET WESTC.

(Named after G. Barker)

This genus is closely related to *Epidendrum;* it differs in that the flat lip lies close to the column but is only united to its edges at the base. The column is always very flat and widened above the middle; the clinandrium is low and not, as in *Epidendrum*, raised behind the anthers.

The ten or more known species all have leafy stems (pseudo-bulbs) with long-stalked, terminal inflorescences whose very pleasing flowers are usually pink. All the species are epiphytes and found only in Central America. Plate 15

Cattleya LDL.

(The genus was set up in 1821 and named after William Cattley) This genus, with its 40 species, is really the finest of all the orchids and each species vies with the others in splendour of colouring and beauty of form. The flowers are amongst the largest in the orchid world and most decorative; they have been greatly improved by hybridisation.

All the species are epiphytes and are found only in America, especially in South and Central America; most of them are warm house plants and not suitable for growing indoors.

The chief characteristics of the flowers is the presence of four pollinia, the only distinction between this genus and *Laelia*. The long stout column, thickened at the end, is very distinct, and is enclosed by the lip as in a tube. The unjointed inflorescence always rises terminally from a flat sheath. The pseudo-bulbs are ovate to cylindrical and stem-like; two, occasionally three, leathery, tongue-shaped leaves are borne on each. Plates 16 to 19

Group 32: *Dendrobiinae*

Dendrobium Sw.

(dendro = tree; bios = to live)

The genus was set up by the Swedish botanist Swartz in 1800. This is a genus rich in species; in 1927 Schlechter gave 900 species distributed over the wide range from Ceylon in a broad belt to Samoa and Tonga, whilst in the northern hemisphere Japan and in the southern New Zealand set the limits.

Not only are there many species but they show great variability so that each of the 900 has its own habit and characteristics. It is not possible to go into these more closely here but it may be mentioned that some are deciduous, others evergreen. Also, as regards temperatures, there are two groups, one requiring tropical, the other subtropical conditions. All are epiphytes though a few also grow on rocks or even on the ground.

The flowers are characterised by the formation of a distinct "chin" and by a comparatively long column with a definite foot and low clinandrium. The projecting anthers have four pollinia. The inflorescence always arises laterally from the pseudo-bulb.

Plates 20 to 23

Group 30: *Laeliinae*

Laelia Ldl.

(Named after the Roman Field Marshall, Laelius)

The 35 species are epiphytes and come from tropical America as well as from Mexico and Brazil.

The presence of 8 pollinia in the anther distinguishes the genus *Laelia* from *Cattleya*; otherwise the species are so similar that they are difficult to distinguish. The growth is sympodial and, on account of the terminal inflorescence, belongs to the Series *Acranthae*. A number of the species are worth growing for the beauty of their flowers; a few can also be grown indoors as, for example. *Laelia anceps* Ldl. which grows in Mexico up to 1000 m

Plates 24 to 26

Brassavola R. Br.
(Named after Dr. Anton M. Brassavola)

The characteristic that distinguishes this genus from the other representatives of the *Laeliinae* group is, as raisers of hybrids know, the long neck at the upper end of the fruit. The genus, which consists of 15 species, is also distinguished by the great horticultural value of *Brassavola digbyana* referred to earlier. All the species of *Brassavola* can be recognised by the thin pseudo-bulbs and fleshy, twisted or cylindrical leaves.

Habitat: all the species occur in tropical America as epiphytes, in an area which extends from Mexico and the West Indies to Southern Brazil, Paraguay and Bolivia. Plate 27

Group 35: *Polystachyinae*
Ansellia Ldl.
(After John Ansell who first found it on the Island of Fernando Po)

The genus *Ansellia,* of which six species are known, is confined to the Continent of Africa. It is one of the few attractive orchids from Africa and, with the large number of flowers in its great panicles — Stein speaks of more than 100 flowers on a metre-high stem — it is a wonderful sight.

The *Polystachyinae* group concludes the genera of *Acranthae,* that is, orchids with terminal inflorescences. All the members of this group have two round pollinia which are often bifid. The Ansellias have tall, rigid stems which are leafy towards the top. The inflorescence is generally loosely many-flowered and branched. The flowers are really attractive, with oblong sepals and petals and a three-lobed lip. Plate 28

Group: 37: *Phajinae*
Calanthe R. Br.
(kalos = beautiful; anthos = flower)

This genus is near *Phajus* though they are very different in appearance. *Calanthe* is distinguished by the distinctly clawed lip and pollinia differently shaped; these are slender, club-shaped and the tips are connate on the sticky disc, which in *Phajus* is differently set; the pollinia are also shorter and thicker.

Calanthes can be divided into two groups; the species in the first group have large pseudo-bulbs, drop their leaves annually and need a definite resting period; the inflorescence arises from the foot of the pseudo-bulb. The second group is usually stemless, evergreen and needs no resting period; the inflorescence springs from the axil of the leaf.

The first group is the most common in cultivation; the long, beautiful free-flowering panicles are good for cutting and the plants can be grown in a room. Most of the plants to-day are hybrids, all originating from *Calanthe vestita*.

Habitat: there are 40 species, all terrestrial, widely distributed from tropical Asia and Australia, across Africa to the West Indies and tropical America.   Plate 29

Chysis LDL.

(chysis = downpour, from the hanging habit)

The genus *Chysis* is distinguished by the 8 remarkable pollinia which are of unequal size and embedded half way up in a mealy, waxy disc. The sepals and petals are very similar and the lateral sepals form a distinct "chin" with the foot of the column. The lip is always three-lobed, with fleshy longitudinal lamellae. The column is usually short, with a fairly long foot. The 6 species are epiphytes of hanging habit.   Plate 30

Phajus LOUR.

(phaios = faded, dark)

The representatives of the genus *Phajus* are large plants and, when in full flower with their metre-long inflorescences, are of imposing appearance. There are about 40 species which grow on the ground in the humus of tropical forests or on the high, grassy savannahs and are distributed over a wide area from West Africa across southern Asia and the Malay Archipelago to Samoa.

From the most closely related genus, *Calanthe*, *Phajus* is distinguished in that the lip has no claw, therefore not stalked and

also not united with the column. Sometimes the lip is spurred, in
a few species the spur is absent. Plate 31

Group 38: *Bulbophyllinae*

Cirrhopetalum LDL.

(cirrhus = shaggy head; petalon = petal)

This genus belongs to a group whose flowers are held in an umbel
and is most remarkable. It is certainly not of great horticultural
valua and its flowers are not decked out in lovely colours, but it
is so charming and its shape so unusual that, on that account,
people are attracted to it as one of the freaks of nature. The
inflorescences are of countless types, resembling tentacles,
spider-like or even like a long paint brush. The labellum is poised
like a see-saw and swings merrily in the wind.

The form of the flower also differs considerably from that of
other genera. For instance, the sepals are very unequal and the
medium sized petals are more or less ciliate. The lip is always
short, tongue-shaped, fleshy, curved and constantly moving for
it is attached to a thin claw on the top of the foot of the column.
The column too, is always short and has a long foot curved at
the top and two indistinct appendages. There are four pollinia.

All the species creep with fairly long rhizomes epiphytically
along the branches of the forest giants of East Africa, Madagascar, tropical Asia, Papua, New Caledonia and Tahitti. Plate 32

Group 42: *Cyrtopodiinae*

Cyrtopodium R. BR.

(kyrtos = crooked; podos = foot)

This genus is closely related to *Eulophia;* there are about 30
species which may be divided in accordance with their mode of
growth into two groups. The first includes the true epiphytes and
these are the best known; the second group includes those which
are terrestrial like the Eulophias, which they resemble in habit.
They are distinguished from the Eulophias by the deciduous bracts
which usually are the same colour as the sepals. A further, important generic character can be seen in the peculiar labellum
which is three-lobed and curved so that the claw ascends with the

two lateral lobes whilst the broad frontal lobe points downwards more or less. The ephyphitic species are interesting and handsome plants which may reach a height of 60 cm; at flowering time they are a wonderful sight. They need the usual compost for epiphytes; leaf-mould and plenty of cow dung may be added. They want plenty of water and heat when growing; later they need a resting period when the leaves are shed.

The terrestrial species should be treated like the Eulophias.

Plate 33

Eulophia R. Br.

(eu = beautiful; lophe = crest)
(This genus was set up by Robert Brown)

According to Schlechter there are about 200 species of this genus, of which 140 occur in Africa; the rest are distributed in America and in India up to the Himalayas. Most of the species are terrestrial, either on steppes or in fairly sunny or shady tropical forests; a few of them are epiphytes. Plate 34

Group 43: *Cymbidiinae*

Cymbidium Sw.

(kymbos = boat; eidos = shape, from the boat-shaped lip)

This genus was set up in 1800 by the Swedish botanist Swartz. The distribution of the 50 or more known species extends from Madagascar across India and Japan to Australia. Most of them are terrestrial, a few only are epiphytic, and many grow as high up as 1800 m in the Himalayas. Their floriferousness and the long-lasting quality of the flowers—they last for weeks—put the Cymbidiums amongst the most popular of the orchids.

The sepals and petals are usually very similar; the lip is about the same size, entire or three-lobed, and has two parallel, blunt keels. The column is slender and hardly curved. The pollinia rest on a short, broad, cross-partition through a square or very short, two-lobed band. The leaves are long, strap-shaped, over-hanging and stiff.

Pseudo-bulbs are not always distinctly formed; if they are

present they are usually so enclosed in tho choathing leaves as
to be hardly recognisable. Plate 35

Group 46: *Catasetinae*

Catasetum RICH.
(kata = down; seta = bristle, referring to the two antenae which
hang down from the column)

This genus is one of the most unusual and fascinating with its
odd-looking flowers; it is striking on account of its peculiar floral
proportions and is matched only by the nearly related *Cycnoches*.

The orchid flowers so far described have all been hermaphrodite
but the species of *Catasetum* are an exception. In one and the same
species plants occur which bear only male flowers, others only
female and also plants which bear male and female flowers in the
same inflorescence. At first, before the unusual floral arrangements
of the genus were sufficiently known, this lead to confusion, which
was increased by the fact that the male flowers were entirely different in shape and colour from the female ones. The latter are
now called the *Monachanthus*- and the male flowers *Myanthus*-
forms. A further characteristic of the male flowers is a mechanism
which has two sensitive antennae, united to the column and
when touched, forcibly ejects the pollinia so that they strike the
back of an insect, where they stick tight.

The pseudo-bulbs are usually spindle-shaped, many-jointed
and enclosed in sheaths. The leaves are usually large, oval, fairly
soft and up to 50 cm long, two and three to a stem; they fall
annually during the dry period, and therefore, all Catasetums
need a complete rest without water. For some unknown reason
nearly all the species of *Catasetum* in cultivation produce male
flowers and hence the female flowers are little known and not
described. Plates 36, 37

Cycnoches LDL.
(kyknos = swan; ochen = neck)

The genus is known as the Swan Orchid because the column of the
male flower is thin and slender, resembling a swan's neck. Not

90

only is it related to *Catasetum* but all the species have the same habit. The sexual organs are the same, there are male, female and hermaphrodite flowers but here two groups can be distinguished; in one the male and female plants resemble each other but in the second group the flowers of the two sexes are differently formed. Their flowers are bizarre and not bright coloured, as in *Catasetum,* but very unusual.

The characteristic distinction between the two genera is that, in *Cycnoches* the inflorescence arises from the axil of an upper leaf on the pseudo-bulb, whilst in *Catasetum* it arises laterally from the base of the pseudo-bulb.

All the 16 known species occur in South and Central America as epiphytes; they are therefore warm house plants. They lose their leaves after flowering and need a long rest when they should not be watered until growth begins again.   Plate 38

Group 47: *Gongorinae*

Stanhopea FROST
(Named after Earl Stanhope)

Of the 50 or more species described by Schlechter, very few have been introduced but those that have been have become popular on account of the peculiar and bizarre structure of the flowers which hang pendent below the plant like butterflies.

The flower stem grows down through the compost and carries 2—10 flowers hanging below. The flowers are very large, strongly scented, white or yellow, often prettily flecked with purple red dots. The sepals are usually broad, the petals tongue-shaped, usually wavy at the edge, both of delicate texture; they become more or less recurved. The labellum is always fleshy and curiously jointed into the hypochil (lower joint), the mesochil (central joint) and the three-lobed epichil (frontal joint). The mesochil normally has two horn-like outgrowths such as are seldom found in the plant world. The column is slender, much winged and the foot gradually merges into the labellum. The pseudo-bulbs are ovate and grooved and have one long, leathery, stalked leaf each.

Habitat: Epiphytes in the forests of Central America.

Plate 39

Group 30: *Laeliinae*

Sophronitis LDL.
(sophron = modest, attractive)

Only seven species are known in this genus, all small epiphytic plants of low growth. A few flower beautifully like the two shown in Plate 40, good plants for the amateur but needing a warm house and not suited to the window sill. Grown on bark they form compact cushions. *S. coccinea* especially is a good plant to grow. By crossing with Cattleyas, wonderful coloured hybrids have been produced which are known under the name "Sophrocattleya".

This genus is easily recognised by its short pseudo-bulbs on a creeping rhizome, each bearing one leaf. The flowers, usually shining scarlet, arise terminally in a one to six flowered, short inflorescence. The sepals and petals are very similar; the lip is not divided and at the base clasps the short column which, with the lip, forms an inconspicuous spur and ends in two ear-like stigmas lobes. There are 8 pollinia in the short anthers. Plate 40

Group 48: *Lycastinae*

Anguloa RUIZ ET PAV.

This species was set up by the Spanish botanists Ruiz and Pavon and named after the Spanish scientist Francisco de Angelo. Nine species are known so far, epiphytes in the Andes of Colombia and Peru and therefore to be regarded as temperate house plants.

They are robust plants with firm pseudo-bulbs which may be 15 cm high and 8 cm across, and carry 2-3 leaves which fall in the resting period that is essential to all the species. The flowers are boat-shaped, always solitary, with a medium long stalk enclosed in bracts. Central sepal and the petals almost equal, oblong, erect; lateral sepals forming a "chin" with the foot of the column. The lip is three-lobed, always smaller than the petals, attached to the tip of the columnar foot and mobile. The column is fairly large and broad with a narrow foot. The flowers, which are strongly aromatic, are of considerable size and unusual shape.

Plate 41

Lycaste LDL.

(From Lycaste, reputedly a town in Crete)

In the genus *Lycaste* the flower is of the attractive, rather bizarre type similar to an Anguloa, to which also it is closely related. The two genera are distinguishable in that in *Lycaste* the sepals are more wide-spread and the labellum is attached to the foot of the column over a wider area and therefore less mobile than in *Anuloa*.

Here too the pseudo-bulbs are more or less ovate; they may carry one or more leaves which are plicate, of rather thinner texture and shed annually during the resting period. The flowers are solidatery on a stem surrounded by bracts.

Habitat: the 35 species that have been described are epiphytes and occur chiefly in the mountains of Central America and in the Andes; a few are found in the mountains of Brazil and the West Indies.

Plates 42, 43

Group 49: *Zygopetalinae*

Zygopetalum HOOK.
(zygon = yoke; petalon = petal)

Zygopetalum is a striking and unique plant which was seldom absent from any orchid collection in former days; it is recommended for warm house treatment. Characteristic of the genus is the short but distinct "chin" formed by the lip with the foot of the column. The sepals and petals are spreading and resemble each other; sometimes the petals are broader. The lip is three-lobed, usually with quite small lateral lobes and a larger, wide, fan-shaped central one; the column is short, hardly thicker at the top, usually hairy in front; the pollinia are attached to a fairly large, sticky disc.

The pseudo-bulbs carry two or more leaves, generally ovate or elliptical. The erect inflorescence, which bears 3-10 fairly large flowers, appears with the young shoot.

About 20 species are known which are distributed all over tropical America, chiefly in Brazil; all are epiphytes.   Plate 44

Group 51: *Maxillarinae*

Maxillaria Ruiz et Pav.

(maxilla = jaw, from the form of the lip)

This genus is characterised by a very distinct development of the foot of the column which, with the lateral petals, forms a "chin". The column is usually straight, moderately long and the hood-shaped anthers contain two pollinia which rest on a broad, sticky mass directly or on a small callus.

There are more than 250 species, all from tropical America, and they exhibit widely different types of growth. Thus some have the pseudo-bulbs closely packed along the rhizome, in others they are much further apart and may be erect stems bearing leaves in two ranks. Yet another group has no pseudo-bulbs and its representatives look like little irises. These epiphytes are of botanical rather than horticultural value but some of the species, in spite of their tropical origin, can be grown in a room if this is fairly warm.   Plates 45, 46

Group 57: *Aspasiinae*

Trichopilia Ldl.

(thrix, trichos = hairy; pilos = cap)

The Tricopiliàs are attractive orchids whose flowers are only medium-sized but, as a rule, freely produced so that they are very suitable for amateur growers. They are epiphytes and are found on trees in the tropical forests from Mexico to Brazil and in the West Indies. The floral characteristics consist in the undivided lip which is trumpet-shaped and rolled round the column, either entirely or at the base only. The inflorescence generally carries several flowers though in a few species they are solitary but in that case rudimentary, undeveloped flowers can be seen.

The pseudo-bulbs may be roundish, ovate or oblong, always laterally compressed, surrounded by the remains of bracts and bearing one leaf each. The leaves are oblong-elliptic, attenuate and usually keeled.   Plate 47

Group 58: *Oncidiinae*

Miltonia LDL.

(Named after John Milton, the poet)

The genus Miltonia is closely related to the Odontoglossums but is distinguished by the short column and the flat lip which stands out at right angles and usually has only a few short ridges. It is also very near *Oncidium* from which it is separated by the large undivided labellum which has no tubercles at the base, only a short crest.

The 20 known species are distributed chiefly in Brazil and Colombia, a few occur in Costa Rica and Paraguay; all are epiphytes. Those from Colombia can be grown cooler than those from Brazil for they have the same habitat as the Cattleyas and live under the same conditions.

Cultivation: Miltonias, with their usually large, attractive flowers, can be used as indoor plants and are most attractive when in flower, but they are no good for cutting.   Plates 48, 49

Odontoglossum H., B. ET K.

(Genus set up by Humboldt, Bonpland and Knuth)

(odontos = tooth; glossa = tongue, from the denticulate lip)

Schlechter gives between 80 and 90 species of *Odontoglossum,* almost all occurring as epiphytes in the high mountain forests of tropical America.

The chief characteristic of the genus is the position of the lip or, rather, the claw of the lip which is almost parallel with the column so that the lamina of the lip stands out at right angles to it. The slender column bears two auricles or wings near the stigma and is never pulvinate at the base. The pseudo-bulbs are always laterally compressed, with one to three leaves at the top. The flowers are carried in erect racemes or pendent panicles.

Plates 50 to 53

Oncidium Sw.

(onkos = hook; eidos = form)

With more than 500 species, this genus has a wide range of forms, amongst them many beautiful and striking plants for the amateur.

Typical of this genus is the position of the labellum which, in contrast to *Odontoglossum*, stands out from the base of the short column and forms a right angle with it. Near the stigma are two small auricles or wing-like appendages on each side. The flowers of this genus are characterised by two spherical or oval, stalked pollinia with which they adhere to a distinct sticky disc.

The inflorescence, which may be as long as 2 m or, in some species, even 3 m long, permits the division of the Oncidiums into two groups; in one the flowers are always normal, similar in shape on the inflorescence. In the other group, on the contrary, the normal flowers are mixed with a number of false flowers which are star-shaped with six to nine radiating structures but without the other floral characters.　　　　Plates 54 to 57

Group 65: *Sarcanthinae*

Angraecum THOU.
(A Malayan name)

The genus is recognised by its very short column with two auricles and a deeply emarginate rostellum; further, the lip has a pouch-like or filamentous spur and the pollinia are either in pairs on one much shortened stalk or on two stalks on the same sticky disc. Since the flower stems arise, several together, laterally from the leaf axils, they belong to the *Pleuranthae* group. About 50 species are known, all epiphytic in tropical Africa and Madagascar.　　　　Plate 58

Euanthe SCHLTR.
(eu = beautiful, true; anthos = flower)

Schlechter has set up a separate genus for this attractive plant, which formerly was included in *Vanda*, on account of its unusual characters; it is the only species in the genus. The exceptionally wide, flat sepals and petals make the flowers look quite different from a *Vanda* but the most characteristic thing is the small labellum which is divided into a very concave hypochil firmly united to the column and an epichil attached which is almost kidney-shaped, with a few keels in the middle. The column is unusually short and merges gradually into the labellum. The hooded anthers contain two round pollinia attached to the centre of an almost linear band of the oval sticky mass.   Plate 59

Phalaenopsis BL. Butterfly Orchid

National flower of the Malays
(phalaina = butterfly; opsis = appearance)

There are more than 40 species in this genus, a few of them having the finest of all the orchid flowers, not so much on account of the especially beautiful colouring but more because of their charming shapes and their delicacy. They want considerable heat because they come from very hot regions such as the Sunda Islands, the Philippines, Burma, Siam and Indochina where they grow epiphytically in a very moist atmosphere. Almost all are stemless but belong to the monopodial orchids.

The chief character of the flowers is the flat lip, without spur or "chin", which is attached to the column.   Plates 60 to 62

Vanda R. BR.
(Vanda is a sanscrit name)

This genus which includes some 45 known species, mostly large plants, have the monopodial form of growth. They are generally tropical epiphytes and occur in the monsoon area of India but are also widely distributed as far as New Guinea.

The generic characteristics are based on the labellum which has several joints. Near the short spur is the hypochil which is prolonged into the epichil. The column is short and thick and generally is further thickened at the base. The hooded anthers contain two pollinia.   Plates 63 to 64

Group 1:
Cypripedilinae

PLATE I

**Paphiopedilum
bellatulum** PFTZ.
(bellatulum =
beautiful)

This charming little plant, belonging to the *Niveum* group, is called the Plover Orchid on account of its spotted, egg-shaped labellum. The tongue-shaped, blunt leaves are dark green with paler blotches on the upper side, dull purple below. The solitary flower is borne on a short stalk, and is white marked with reddish-brown flecks which are closer together towards the base of the flower. The sepals are almost circular, the petals elliptic. The labellum is comparatively small, egg-shaped with small dots. The columnat disc is of the same colour and almost circular.

Flowering period: in spring. Habitat: Chan States (western Central Asia) and Burma. Introduced in 1883 by Low. Warm house.

97

PLATE 2

**Paphiopedilum
curtisii** Pftz.

THIS is one of the variegated-leaved Lady's Slippers and can be used as a cut flower. Its lanceolate, elliptical leaves, 20 cm long, up to 5 cm wide, are indistinctly marbled in pale and dark green and are usually four in number. The flower is solitary and the stem carries a spathe-like bract below the ovary. The flower, about 10 cm across, has a short, broadly ovate, pointed green standard, bordered with white and with purple longitudinal stripes; the back is streaked with purple. The petals are greenish-pink at the base, paler towards the tip, thickly strewn with little dark purple dots. The labellum is greenish-purple-brown, the incurved edge of the lip is pale purple with purple tubercles. The columnar disc is wide and kidney-shaped.

Flowering period: April to July. Habitat: Bovenlands of Padang in Sumatra, at a height of 700 m on limestone.

Cultivation: All the species of Paphioledilum with variegated leaves need warm house treatment, 20° C in winter. Although terrestrial orchids, they want an open compost so should have osmunda and sphagnum, that is the mixture for epiphytes, to which is added leaf-mould, turfy or other good loam. Warm house.

Group 1:
Cypripedilinae

PLATE 3

**Paphiopedilum
insigne** PFTZ.
var. **sanderae**
RCHB. f.

This variety is regarded as an albino, of which several others occur in the genus, e.g. *P. lawrenceanum* var. *hyeanum*.

The type species, *P. insigne*, is the most popular and worthwhile of the orchids. The duration of the flowers, both on the plant and when cut, is unusual; if kept cool it flowers for nearly two months. It is also one of the best orchids for indoor cultivation and seldom fails.

The leaves, from many shoots, are bunched 5-6 together, strap-shaped and linear. The flowers are always solitary, about 8-10 cm across on a stem 20 cm high. The upper sepal, the standard, is roundish, yellowish-green, with green stripes and white on the tip. The petals, which slope downwards, are blunt, yellowish green veined with brown; the labellum is also yellowish-green flushed with brown.

P. insigne var. *sanderae*, on the contrary, has transparent, pale yellow flowers, the tips being white. The standard is striped in pale green. This, and the fact that it flowers freely, makes this variety valuable, especially for cutting. It occurs in the Khasya mountains of Nepal and was introduced to England in 1819.

Cultivation: Although terrestrial, it requires the usual compost for epiphytes with the addition of dried cow dung and ground horn. The type and the variety are both cool house plants but tolerate room temperatures.

99

PLATE 4

**Paphiopedilum
rothschildianum**
Pftz.
(Named in honour
of the great orchid
grower, Rothschild)

This is an attractive Lady's Slipper, very handsome with its tall stems.
It belongs to a small group of this genus characterised by having several
flowers on one stem; the very beautiful *P. philippense* Pftz. also belongs
here and very good hybrids have been raised by crossing with *P. rothschildianum.*

The strap-shaped leaves are shining green and may be as much as 60 cm
long and 5 cm wide. The reddish-brown, hairy peduncle reaches 70 cm
and carries 3-7 flowers, each 13 cm across. The standard is ovate, pointed,
yellowish, striped with dark purple. The lower sepal is similar but shorter
The narrow, linear, tapering petals hang obliquely downwards and are
much twisted, pale green with purple stripes, flecked at the base and with
black bristly tubercles along the edges. The labellum is pale purple with
darker veins; the broad wedge-shaped columnar disc is yellowish and
hairy.

P. rothschildianum was introduced by the firm of Sander in 1888 and
comes from Sumatra and Borneo. Flowering period: July to September.

Cultivation: This is a warm house plant and not suitable for indoor
cultivation; dried cow dung should be added to the usual compost for
epiphytes.

PLATE 5

**Paphiopedilum
sanderianum**
PFTZ.
(Named after
Sander, the well-
known orchid
grower)

This is a very rare species, of fantastic appearance, whose two long petals look almost like shoe laces. The illustration is taken from *Reichenbachia* from a plant grown in England. It belongs to the group with several flowers on the peduncle. The strap-shaped leaves are up to 20 cm long and 4 cm wide. The 50 cm-high flower stem, hairy and reddish brown, carries purple bracts and 3-7 flowers. The standard is long, ovate, pointed, bright yellow with many brownish red stripes. The lower sepal is some-what smaller but similar in colour. The two lateral petals are narrow, ribbon-like, pendant, up to 60 cm long, yellowish with dark brown horizontal stripes, usually twisted. The unusually large, long labellum projects and looks like a slipper; thus the column with its oval disc is exposed, not enclosed as in most species. The labellum is yellowish at the base and purplish red or brown on the "shoe". Flowering period: from February to April.

Cultivation: Although it comes from the Philippines it is a warm house plant. The compost should be the same as for all the species of this genus.

PLATE 6

**Paphiopedilum
venustum** PFTZ.
(venustum =
charming)

THIS is indeed a charming species and also the oldest one known; it was discovered in 1816 by Wallich in Sylhet. According to Schlechter it occurs in the Himalayas at 1000-1500 m. It is decorative when in flower and suitable for indoor cultivation.

The leaves are prettily marbled in dark and light green, the underside flushed with purple; they are strap-shaped and pointed. The peduncle is about 15 cm high and carries an attractive, solitary flower, about 8 cm across. The standard is broadly oval, pointed, white with dark green stripes. The petals stand out horizontally, are widened towards the tip and ciliate; the base is green with black tubercles changing to purple brown in front. The comparatively small labellum is almost cylindrical, bright yellow green suffused with red and veined with green. The columnar disc or staminode is crescent-shaped and yellowish green. Flowering period: in winter from November onwards.

Cultivation: *P. venustum* is a cool house plant and very good for growing in a room. The compost should be that for epiphytes with the addition of dung, as for the other species.

Group 3:
Disaeinae

PLATE 7

Disa uniflora BERG.
(syn. *Disa grandi-
flora* L.f.)

THE best known and most colourful is *Disa uniflora* which grows at the Cape in damp soil among rocks on Table Mountain.

The fleshy roots are finger-like, the leaves tongue-shaped; they form a rosette at first which disappears as the 60 cm-high flower stem rises, carrying the leaves with it. The flowers, solitary or up to five, are very large 9-10 cm across; the broad, scarlet, lateral sepals are delicately poised and held horizontally. The central petal which stands up like a helmet, has a short spur and is bright red on the outside, white to yellow inside and prettily veined with red. The lip is small, narrow, tongue-shaped with the tip recurved.

To prevent its extermination the Government of the Union of South Africa has put *Disa* on the list of "protected plants", hence it is rarely obtainable. Temperate house.

Group 30:
Laeliinae

PLATE 8

**Epidendrum
schomburgkii** LDL.
(After R. Schom-
burgk, formerly
Director of the Bo-
tanic Gardens,
Adelaide)

PLATE 8

**Epidendrum
radicans**
LDL. et PAV.
(radicans =
rooting)

Left E. radicans

THIS is a tall shrubby plant, up to 3 m high; its slender stems produce aerial roots freely and these also serve for anchorage. The flowers would not be particularly striking were it not for their brilliant, almost luminous, orange red colour. The stems are closely set, sometimes in two ranks, with small oval leaves, notched at the tip. The uniform-coloured flowers are bunched on a long, bare peduncle; sepals and petals are similar in shape and radiating; the labellum has three lobes, the two lateral ones being prettily fringed whilst the wedge-shaped central lobe is deeply cleft.

Cultivation: The plant flowers the whole year through, even when young, so that it can be used in a room. Habitat: Mexico and Guatemala. Temperate house.

Right (above) E. schomburgkii

THIS species is similar to the preceding one but its roundish, stouter stem, also with the leaves in two ranks, is barely 30 cm high. The leaves are oblong, blunt-tipped, almost fleshy, evergreen also like the preceding, often flecked with red and about 9 cm long. The luxuriant terminal raceme is fairly long, bare, with bracts at the upper part; the flowers are about 3 cm across, of a striking, shining scarlet colour. The sepals and petals are
continued page 161

Group 30:
Laeliinae

**Epidendrum
cooperianum**
BATEM.
(Named after
T. Cooper)

THIS species has bulbless, slender stems up to 80 cm high, which bear charming, pendent racemes. The individual flowers are fairly small but by their numbers and their beautiful pink colour, produce a noteworthy effect. It is a warm house plant, not suitable for indoor cultivation.

The fairly stout stems are compressed above, with the leaves in two ranks; the leaves are lanceolate with long points, stiff and leathery. The terminal inflorescence may reach a length of 15-20 cm and carry 10-25 flowers which are about 4 cm across and a bright pale pink. The sepals and petals are oblong, spreading, yellowish green, the petals being narrower than the sepals. The labellum is three-lobed and a beautiful rose pink; the lateral lobes are wider than the central one.

Flowering period: April to May. Habitat: Brazil. The compost should be that recommended for epiphytes. Warm house.

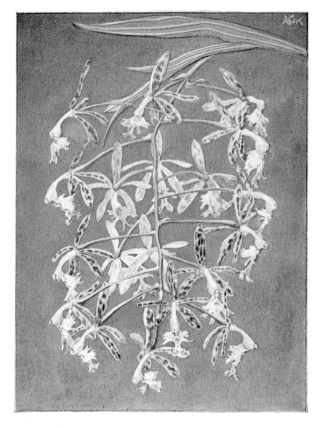

PLATE 10

**Epidendrum
raniferum** LDL.
(raniferum = frog-
like, referring to
the shape of the
labellum)

THIS is a magnificent plant for the amateur's greenhouse. Its stem-like pseudo-bulbs reach about 60 cm in height and in the upper part are laxly leafy. The leaves are tongue-shaped and up to 25 cm long. The many-flowered inflorescence is terminal and pendent. The small flowers are yellowish-green sprinkled with small purple dots. The sepals and petals are wide-spread, oblong, the sepals somewhat wider than the narrow petals. The labellum, attached to the white column, has a six-lobed lip and is yellowish with purple flecks. Temperate house.

Flowering period: June to August. Habitat: Brazil. Needs the usual compost for epiphytes.

Group 26:
Pleurothallidinae

PLATE II

**Masdevallia
backhousiana**
RCHB. f.
(Named after
J. Backhouse)

Tʜɪs is a rare variety of the well-known *M. chimaera* Rchb.f. which has the same habit but the flower differs in the much broader sepals and in the colour; the ochre yellow ground bears large purple-red flecks and the inner surface is covered with felted hairs. The petals are very small, oblong-wedge-shaped, pale to yellowish. The labellum is small and almost shoe-shaped.

Flowering period: November to February. Habitat: Colombia.

Cultivation: Owing to the delicate roots, polypodium, sphagnum and dried cow dung should be added to the usual compost for epiphytes. Masdevallias do not need a resting period. Cool house.

PLATE 12

**Masdevallia
shuttleworthii**
Rchb. f.
(Named after
Mr. Shuttleworth)

This very unassuming species is a contrast to the more beautiful and interesting *M. backhousiana*; the leaves are tufted, short-stalked, elliptical and pointed: the solitary flowers are on stems 10-12 cm high. The pretty little flower is of a more tubular type, which is occasionally found in the genus, but can always be recognised by the three slender appendages. The three sepals form a short, stumpy tube; the upper sepal is erect, curved like a hood, bright yellow and pink with a few wine-red stripes. The two lower ones are ovate, slanting downwards, pink with many purple red spots. Whilst the upper sepal narrows suddenly to form a slender "tail", the two lower sepals are gradually drawn out to a length of 5 cm; they are green at the base and orange yellow above.

Flowering period: April to August. Habitat: Colombia, in the Andes at 2000-2600 m. Cultivation as for the preceding species. Cool house.

Group 28:
Coelogyninae

PLATE 13

**Coelogyne
cristata** Ldl.
(cristatus = crest-
bearing, referring
to the crest on the
lip)

This species was introduced in 1837 from Nepal by Dr. Wallich; it also occurs in Sikkim and the Himalayas and is usually found as a terrestrial orchid at heights of 1500-2500 m.

The pseudo-bulbs are spherical to egg-shaped, 6 cm long and 4 cm in diameter, of a bright green colour. They become somewhat wrinkled in the resting period but should not be allowed to shrivel up. There are two leaves to each bulb, narrowly lanceolate and running to a sharp point. The flower stem, which arises from a special short shoot, develops into a many-flowered, arching spray. The flowers are comparatively large, snow white, delicately scented and each has a pale brown bract below. The sepals and petals are fairly wide, the edges wavy and the tip recurved. The lip is three-lobed with five fringed yellow strips; the central lobe is blunt and curved backwards.

Flowering period: January to April. Very beautiful when in full flower and suitable for bouquets, etc.

Cultivation: A cool house plant, not requiring much heat and therefore suitable for indoor cultivation.

PLATE 14

**Coelogyne
speciosa** LDL.
(speciosus =
showy)

ALTHOUGH this species is of no use for cutting, it is a good plant for amateurs and for indoor cultivation. It comes from tropical regions but on
high mountains and is therefore a temperate house orchid.

The pseudo-bulbs are egg-shaped, somewhat angular, about 5 cm high
and carry only one leaf each. The leaves are broadly elliptic, plicate along
the veins, up to 20-25 cm long. The short flower stem appears at the same
time as the young leaf and, as a result of the weight of the one or two
flowers, hangs downwards.

The flowers are below the leaves and are large, up to 15 cm across and
greenish yellow. The sepals are oblong, wider in the upper half; the upper
sepal is hooded and bent forward. The two bright green petals are very
narrow and linear, prettily waved and more or less recurved. The large
labellum is three-lobed, the central lobe sharply toothed along the edge;
the inside is veined and dotted with red or chestnut brown and has two
long brown double crests and one shorter.

Flowering period: April to July. Habitat: Malaya, Sumatra, Java on
mountains at a height of 1000-15000 m.

Cultivation: should be treated as an epiphyte as regards compost.
Coelogynes are evergreen plants but need a resting period after flowering.

Group 30:
Laeliinae

PLATE 15

Barkeria spectabilis
Batem.
(spectabilis =
worth seeing)

THE stems of this really fine plant may be as much as 15 cm high, cylindrical and bearing two leaves. The leaves are somewhat fleshy, lanceolate and pointed. The long terminal peduncle carries large flowers 8-10 cm across. According to Schlechter the flowers are rose pink, to Stein pale pink, whilst the flowers in the illustration which is taken from the English original, shows them as white; evidently the colour in this species is very variable, which is not unusual amongst orchids. The sepals and petals are similar in shape; the lip is ovate elliptic, white with small red dots.

Flowering period: July to September. Habitat: Guatemala. Warm house.

PLATE 16

**Cattleya
bowringiana**
VEITCH
(Named after
J. C. Bowring)

THIS species belongs to a special group whose inflorescences are many flowered and articulated into the main axis, to which belong also *C. guttata* Ldl. and *C. skinneri* Ldl. Even if the flowers are small, they give a wonderful effect owing to their number.

C. bowringiana is a magnificent plant which develops into a real show specimen. The long pseudo-bulbs are compressed, the several joints arising from sheaths; they attain a height of 60 cm and bear two leaves each, which are broadly lanceolate, firm and grey green. The tall peduncle may have as many as twenty flowers. The individual flowers are 6-8 cm across and vary in colour from pinkish-violet to a warm purple violet. The sepals are lanceolate with blunt points, the petals broader, ovate and obtuse. The labellum is comparatively small, three-lobed, golden yellow in the throat, pale pink to pink in front. The whole flower is decorated with fine dark veining.

Flowering period: September to December. Habitat: British Honduras. Warm house.

Group 30:
Laeliinae

PLATE 17

Cattleya citrina
LDL.
(citrina = lemon
yellow)

THIS species is unique of its kind; all the rules seem to have been turned topsy turvey. Not only are the flowers pendent but the whole plant hangs down; the shoots and leaves turn away from the sun in contradistinction to most plants which are heliotropic. This alone makes the species interesting enough but, added to this, is the grey green colour of the leaves which occur in pairs on the ovate pseudo-bulbs. The pleasantly scented, lemon yellow, solitary flowers are long-stalked but barely overtop the leaves. The sepals are oblong and blunt, the petals rather wider and wavy. The labellum is trumpet-shaped, the edge of the lip always crisply wavy, sometimes bright yellow. More rarely the tulip-like flower has golden yellow dots on the lip.

Flowering period: October to April. Habitat: Mexico.

Cultivation: Warm house plant: needs a light position close against the glass. It is best grown on cork.

Group 30:
Laeliinae

PLATE 18

Cattleya dowiana
BATEN
var. **aurea**
T. MOORE
(Named after
J. M. Dow;
aurea = golden)

IN comparison with the preceding species, *C. dowiana* var. *aurea* is a real jewel in its magnificent colouring; unfortunately it has always been rare but its good breeding qualities have resulted in many hybrids. It is invaluable for decoration but not as a cut flower since it lasts for only a short time.

The difference between *C. dowiana* and the variety *aurea* is in a warmer yellow lip and a richer patterning of golden veins; bearing in mind its habitat, it is doubtful whether the one should be considered a variety of the other. *C. dowiana* comes from Costa Rica, whilst var. *aurea* is known only in Colombia; to-day at all events, no connecting link is known between the habitat of the type species and that of the variety in Colombia. Obviously the relation between them is very close but they can only be united on the assumption that, at one time, they had a common habitat.

In habit it resembles *C. labiata* and hence *C. dowiana* is placed in the *Labiatae* section which contains other species such as *C. gaskelliana*, *C. mendlii*, *C. mossiae*, etc. *C. dowiana* var. *aurea* is smaller than *C. labiata*, especially in the flower. Warm house.

Group 30:
Laeliinae

PLATE 19

**Cattleya
warscewiczii**
Rchb. f.
(syn. *C. gigas*
Lind. et Andre)
(Named after
J. Warscewicz, of
the Botanic Gar-
dens, Cracow)

This species is often called *C. gigas*, perhaps because it is easier to pronounce; but since Schlechter gave the other name earlier, it has priority according to the Rules of Nomenclature.

This is a very strong-growing species whose flowers are amongst the largest in the genus. The rigid but distinguished poise of the flowers as well as their beauty of colouring makes this one of the best of the Cattle-yas; unfortunately it is not so good for cutting since it flowers in summer. It also belongs to the *Labiatae* section. The pseudo-bulbs are flat, spindle-shaped, jointed, up to 30 cm long and bear only one leaf which is very leathery, oblong, bluntly rounded and about 30 cm long. The inflorescence may carry up to 10 flowers, which may be as much as 20 cm across. The three erect sepals are narrowly lanceolate and, like the petals, pale violet pink; the latter, also erect, are wedge-shaped at the base, rather wider in front and crenulate. The labellum is tubular in the throat, two-lobed, prominant and beautifully waved at the edge; the colour is a lovely dark reddish purple with paler veins and a conspicuous yellow blotch on each side of the throat.

Cultivation: warm house. Habitat: near Medellin, Colombia. Flowering period: July to August.

PLATE 20

**Dendrobium
chrysotoxum**
WALL.
(gold coloured)

THE pseudo-bulbs are slender, spindle shaped and with several joints bearing at the end two or three leathery, oval, shortly pointed, evergreen leaves. The plant is striking on account of its sparse foliage for usually only the bulbs of the preceding year bear leaves. The scented, arching sprays, about 20 cm long, bearing 8 to 15 flowers of a lovely golden yellow, arise laterally, chiefly from the upper end of the pseudo-bulbs. The petals are much broader than the sepals; the almost circular labellum is velvety, often with dark brown blotches in the throat; the edge is finely notched.

Flowering period: November to about April. Habitat: Burma and Yunnan. Warm house.

Group 32:
Dendrobiinae

Dendrobium nobile
LDL.
(nobile = distin-
guished, noble)

THIS is a quite outstanding and lovely plant which comes from the Himalayas where it is epiphytic though occasionally growing on rocks.

The stem-like pseudo-bulb is up to 45 cm long, many-jointed, many-leaved and clothed with membranous, whitish leaf-sheaths. The leaves are lanceolate, bluntish and alternate, in two ranks; they usually fall in the resting period. At the upper nodes of the stem the two to four-flowered inflorescences arise on comparatively short stalks. The flower is pink on a white or yellowish ground, flushed with deeper purple towards the ends of the petals and sepals. The flower is scented and about 7 cm across; the labellum surrounds the column like a trumpet, the lobe is almost circular, velvety, with a dark purple blotch at the throat.

Flowering period: March to June. Habitat: Himalayas to Yunnan. Temperate house plant; it needs the usual compost for epiphytes and is suitable for cultivation indoors, where it makes a wonderful show.

Group 32:
Dendrobiinae

PLATE 22

**Dendrobium
phalaenopsis**
Fitzg.
(phalaina = but-
terfly,
opsis = ap-
pearance)

Wɪᴛʜ its variety *schroederianum*, this is the most outstanding and valuable species in the genus as regards the flowers and their value for cutting.

The fine flowers are almost unsurpassable in their compactness of form and beauty of colour. The lasting qualities and the long-stemmed inflorescence make it an ideal flower for orchid growers. As the specific name indicates, it is similar to the genus *Phalaenopsis*; the flowers closely resemble each other.

Strong plants reach a height of 70 cm. The pseudo-bulbs are jointed, the joints being club-shaped, and bear at the top a number of evergreen leaves which are flat, leathery and oblong. The terminal inflorescence is slender, 55 cm long and bears 4 to 12 flowers. These are about 8 cm across; the ground colour is white, flushed with rose pink becoming darker towards the edge; in var. *schroederianum* the colour is paler or darker cherry red; the darker it is, the more valuable the plant. The petals are broader than the sepals. The labellum has a pronounced "chin" and a long pointed frontal lobe; at the base it is spurred and the throat is a dark purple with darker purple veining below.

Flowering period: January to May. Habitat: Queensland, Timor, New Guinea. It is a warm house plant and needs the usual compost for epiphytes.

118

PLATE 23

**Dendrobium
pierardi** Roxb.
(Name of unknown
origin)

When in full flower, this is an enchanting plant. When old enough, the long, stem-like pseudo-bulbs become pendent and are then leafless during the resting period but then the many flowers look wonderful, the whole plant is like a little waterfall. It cannot be used as a cut flower for that would mean removing the whole pseudo-bulb which would greatly weaken the plant. It is a good plant for amateurs but requires warm house treatment.

The pseudo-bulbs reach a length of a metre; they are round, much jointed, with leaves set closely in two ranks. *D. pierardi* belongs to the group which drop their leaves in the resting period; they are lanceolate, pointed and thin in texture.

The flowers arise in clusters from the nodes of the stem; they are short-stalked and may be solitary or three together. The individual flowers are about 4.5 cm across; the sepals and petals are pale pink, almost 2.5 cm long, the petals a little wider. The trumpet-shaped labellum has a broad, oval, pale yellow frontal lobe, prettily veined in red at the rear, the edge being fimbriated.

Flowering period: April and May. Habitat: Burma and the Himalayas in warm, moist valleys.

Cultivation: Dendrobiums should usually be put in small pots so that in summer, which is their chief growing time, they must be watered often and freely. Warm house.

Group 30:
Laeliinae

PLATE 24

Laelia flava LDL.
(flava = pure
yellow)

Laelia cinnabarina
BATEM.
(cinnabarina =
cinnabar red)

Below: L. cinnabarina

THIS species has slender, cylindrical pseudo-bulbs, each bearing a single leaf, jointed and covered with membranous sheats. The leaf is lanceolate, pointed, fleshy, leathery and up to 25 cm long. The loose inflorescence, up to 30 cm long, is not jointed and bears 3 to 7 beautiful, orange red flowers about 8 cm across. Sepals and petals are similar in shape, linear-lanceolate, pointed at the tip; the labellum is deeply three-lobed, orange red with darker veins and three keels; the lateral lobes are lanceolate to triangular, the central one crisply wavy with the tip recurved.

Flowering period: February to May. Habitat: Brazil. Warm house.

It has no horticultural value and is just a plant for amateurs where a greenhouse is available.

All Laelias must have a resting period after flowering but too great shrinkage of the pseudo-bulbs should be avoiled. Compost as for epiphytes.

Above: L. flava

ALTHOUGH the flower of *L. flava* is only medium-sized, yet its yellow colour and good appearance makes it quite a useful *Laelia*. The pseudo-bulbs are 5 to 12 cm high, narrowly cylindrical and bear one leaf each. It may here be said that the stem-like pseudo-bulbs of orchids usually become rather longer in cultivation than on imported plants that have been grown under favourable conditions and with more light than we, with our feebler sunlight, can give them. The reverse is the case with those

continued page 161

120

Group 30:
Laeliinae

PLATE 25

Laelia purpurata
LDL.
(purpurata =
flushed with
purple)

THIS species, like the others in the genus, is an epiphyte of the sympodial type. The pseudo-bulbs are jointed, slender and club-shaped, flattened, grooved and up to 60 cm long, bearing one leaf each; the leaves are thick and leathery, slender tongue-shaped and crenate. It belongs to the *Acranthae* and has a terminal inflorescence with 3 to 5 flowers which are 16 cm across, the lip being of wonderful form and colour. Sepals oblong, pointed, white flushed with pink; the petals are narrow elliptic, wavy, pointed, otherwise similar to the sepals. The three-lobed lip surrounds the column; the front lobe is broad, smooth and dark purple with darker veining; the edge of the lip is rather paler and prettily waved; the colour of the throat is yellow.

Flowering period: May to June. Habitat: Brazil.

Numerous hybrids with *Brassovola digbyana* Ldl. have been successfully raised and with their very beautiful fringed and fimbriated lip and lovely scent have lead to the large-flowered generic hybrids, the *Brassolaeliocattleyas*.

L. purpurata is not suitable for indoor cultivation but strongly recommended for the amateur with a greenhouse. Warm house.

PLATE 26

Laelia tenebrosa
ROLFE
(tenebrosa = dark,
gloomy, on account
of the colour)

THIS beautiful, large-flowered species with its warm shades of colour, has also been used for hybridisation with species of *Cattleya*.

The pseudo-bulbs, up to 25 cm high, are club-shaped and have only one leaf which is tongue-shaped, leathery and up to 25 cm long. In habit it closely resembles *Laelia grandis* Ldl. et Paxt. but the flowers are larger about 16 cm across and arise from the floral bract in a short, three-to four-flowered inflorescence. The sepals and petals are spreading, almost equal in length, of a more or less dark yellow brown colour, though the sepals are slightly narrower and wavy at the edges, their tips recurved, whilst the petals are broader, wavy and folded backwards. The three-lobed lip is a wonderful purple violet; the two lateral lobes form a long tube round the column which expands like a trumpet into a broadly oval central lobe. The edge of the lip is wavy, recurved and indented. The laterals may have a white base and, together with the central lobe, are finely veined with deep violet.

Flowering period: May and June. Habitat: Brazil and Bahia.

Cultivation: The Laelias require the same treatment as Cattleyas, that is, compost for epiphytes with the addition of osmunda and sphagnum.

PLATE 27

Brassavola nodosa
Ldl.
(nodosa = knotted)

THIS very distinct species shows clearly how orchids can adapt themselves to their surroundings by means of their narrowly cylindrical leaves. The striking transformation which reduces the breadth of a leaf, indicates that in its native land the plant is exposed to strong sun and drying winds. The leaves are up to 15 cm long and are in tufts; the upper side is sometimes a little flattened. The peduncle bears several white flowers; the lip is trumpet-shaped with an expanded lobe.

Flowering period: October to December. Habitat: the West Indies and Central America. Warm house.

PLATE 28

Ansellia africana
LDL.

THIS species, together with *A. nilotica* N.E. Br. which it much resembles, is the best known of the type with sympodial growth. It has cylindrical, grooved, jointed pseudo-bulbs up to 60 cm long and bearing 4-7 leaves which are up to 30 cm long, linear, pointed, five-veined and united with the spathe that surrounds the stem. The loose, many-flowered panicle is about 40 cm long; the flowers are yellowish flecked with chocolate brown and about 3 cm across; the sepals and petals are oblong, blunt, the latter are the wider. The labellum is three-lobed with three low keels and short, blunt lateral lobes. The central lobe is oblong, blunt and with golden keels. According to Stein, it grows near the coast on the ground but is also epiphytic. Temperate house.

Group 37:
Phajinae

PLATE 29

Calanthe vestita
L̲D̲L̲. var. **regnieri**
V̲E̲I̲T̲C̲H̲
(vestita = clothed)

T̲H̲E̲ pseudo-bulbs are elongated, ovate, thick, blunt-angled and up to 10 cm long. The leaves, which drop at flowering time, are lanceolate, pointed and about 4.5 cm long. The many-flowered, hairy peduncle is almost a metre long and arches over; the white flowers are about 6 cm across. The sepals and petals are elliptical, pointed, slightly recurved and up to 3.5 cm long. The lip is broad and four-lobed, orange-yellow at the base, rose pink in front with a darker blotch in the throat.

Flowering period: November and December. Habitat: Cochin China. Compost as for terrestrial orchids. Temperate house.

PLATE 30

Chysis bractescens
LDL.
(bractescens =
having bracts)

THE pseudo-bulbs are spindle-shaped, fleshy, jointed and bear three to five leaves which are large, pointed oval, much pleated and drop in the resting period. The inflorescence appears with the young shoots; it arises from the axil of one of the lower leaves and bears three to eight flowers. The large flowers, about 8 cm across, are waxy, ivory white and of a pleasant, compact shape. The two lateral sepals are broadly triangular at the base, whilst the upper sepal and the petals are narrower and more like each other. The labellum is three-lobed, golden yellow patterned with red inside, with two fleshy lamellae.

Flowering period: April and May. Habit and cultivation: *Chysis bractescens* is an epiphyte and grows in Mexico. On account of its pendent habit it should be grown on cork or in a wooden basket. Warm house.

126

Group 37:
Phajinae

PLATE 31

**Phajus
tankervilliae** BL.
(Named after
Emma, Lady
Tankerville)
(syn. *P. grandifo-
lius* LDL.)

THE ovate pseudo-bulbs are up to 7 cm in diameter and bear three to
four leaves. The leaves are oblong-lanceolate, pointed, the base long and
narrow, about 60 cm long. The flowers are 10 cm across, loosely arranged
in a metre-long panicle. The rather similar, pointed sepals and petals are
wide-spread, white outside and brown within. The labellum has a long tube
with a short spur, white in front, the tube with purple veins, the throat
yellow.

Flowering period: May to July.

From its habitat *P. tankerville* should be a warm house plant; it comes
from India and the Malay Archipelago where it is often found on grassy
savannahs. Nevertheless it needs the same compost as terrestrial orchids,
made more open with osmunda and polypodium as well as turf and sand.
It appreciates dried cow dung or horn meal.

PLATE 32

**Cirrhopetalum
makoyanum**
RCHB. f.

THIS species has ovate, wrinkled, furrowed pseudo-bulbs, 4 cm high and 2-6 cm apart on the creeping rhizome. Leaves solitary, oblong, tongue-shaped, attenuated at the base, about 14 cm long. The flower stalk is thin, wiry, dark brown and may be as much as 25 cm long. The flowers are very narrow, yellowish with fine brownish-red dots and about 3.5 cm long. The central sepal and the petals are ciliate, the labellum is very small.

Flowering period: January and February. Habitat: India. Warm house.

Group 42:
Cyrtopodiinae

PLATE 33

**Cyrtopodium
andersonii** R. Br.
(Named after
Anderson,
Director of the
Botanic Gardens,
Calcutta)

THE pseudo-bulbs, which reach a height of 60 cm, are thick, spindle-shaped and bear several leaves which are narrowly lanceolate, about 50 cm long and attenuated. The flower stem is up to 120 cm high, much branched, many-flowered and bears yellowish-green bracts. The sepals and the somewhat spatulate petals are spreading, broadly elliptic, greeish yellow and about 2.5 cm long. The labellum is three-lobed, golden yellow or orange; the lateral lobes stand erect and the short frontal lobe is crisply waved.

Flowering period: April and May. Habitat: West Indies. Warm house.

PLATE 34

**Eulophia
guineensis** LDL.

As its specific name indicates, this plant comes from Guinea on the coast of West Africa where it lives in humus in tropical forests. It is a handsome plant while many of the species have only small flowers.

The pseudo-bulbs are thick, ovate, up to 5 cm high and bear two or three petiolate leaves, elliptical in shape, attenuate and up to 25 cm long. The inflorescence is about 50 cm high, bearing 5 to 15 loosely arranged flowers. The petals and sepals are narrow, tongue-shaped, greenish flushed with dark purple and veined; they are recurved and stand erect like a crest. The spurred lip is trumpet-shaped and three-lobed, the throat greenish white; the frontal lobe is semicircular, prettily waved on the edge, rose pink striped with carmine towards the base.

Flowering period: April and May.

As a terrestrial orchid from the forests this species needs plenty of half-rotted beech leaf-mould mixed with polypodium and osmunda fibre and a little river sand and also some turfy loam. Manure can also be given. Warm house.

Group 43:
Cymbidiinae

PLATE 35

**Cymbidium
lowianum** RCHB. f.
(Named after
Sir Hugh Low)

THIS species has a short, thickened stem which bears 6-8 leaves, linear, pointed firm in texture and up to 75 cm long. The long flower stem arches over and carries 10-12 flowers laxly arranged. The flowers are about 10 cm across and last a long time. The spreading sepals and petals are greenish-yellow and about 5.5 cm long. The labellum is three-lobed and yellow with a shining scarlet frontal lobe.

Flowering period: February to July. Habitat: Burma.

Cultivation: This species is very suitable for cultivation in a room, if the window sill is a wide one. It needs temperate house treatment. Only well-rooted plants are certain to flower, so they should not be re-potted too often; it is better to give them manure.

PLATE 36

**Catasetum
macrocarpum**
Rich.
(macro = huge;
carpum = fruit)

THE male inflorescence bears 4 to 10 flowers and is about 45 cm high. The sepals and petals slope downwards, are greenish with red dots, attenuate and up to 4.5 cm long. Lip yellow, helmet-shaped with rounded lateral lobes and with three humps on the frontal lobe. The column is green and has two thread-like antennae. The female flower, on the other hand, is borne on a similar inflorescence; the sepals and petals are oval, only about 2 cm long, shortly attenuate; the lip is open, tall helmet-shaped, yellow inside; the column is short and without antennae.

Flowering period: October to December. Warm house.

Group 46:
Catasetinae

PLATE 37

Catasetum tabulare
Lᴅʟ.
(= table-like)

Tʜᴇ pseudo-bulbs are spindle-shaped, jointed, about 15 cm long. The leaves are broadly lanceolate, 5 cm wide and 30 cm long, dark on the upper side, pale green below. The flower stalk is 50 cm long and arches over, bearing 2-6 flowers about 10 cm across. The sepals and petals are narrowly linear, pointed, 5.5 cm long, greenish-yellow in colour, white towards the base on the upper side more or less flushed with pink and with red dots. The labellum is oblong, blunt with a short pouch below the middle, on the upper side with an ovate, whitish thickened disc which includes almost the whole surface of the lip. The whitish-green, helmet-shaped column, dotted with red on the outside, shows between the two antennae which are easily recognisable on the disc and make it clear that this is a male flower; although the entrance to the stigma is visible, the stigma remains infertile. The female flower is unknown.

Flowering period: April to September. Habitat and cultivation: There are some 150 species of *Catasetum* distributed throughout tropical America and all are epiphytes; they are therefore no good as indoor plants but anyone with a greenhouse should have one or two representatives of these interesting orchids. They are not of much horticultural value and generally only to be seen in Botanic Gardens.

Group 46:
Catasetinae

PLATE 38

**Cycnoches
chlorochilum** KL.
(chlor = green;
chilos = lipped)

THIS species has spindle-shaped pseudo-bulbs up to 30 cm high; the plicate, elliptical leaves may be as long as 40 cm; they are two-ranked, the sheaths closely surrounding the stem. *C. chlorochilum* belongs to the group in which the male and female flowers are similar. The flowers are spreading, 15 cm wide and yellowish-green. The labellum has blackish green flecks at the base and is green in front and pouched.

Flowering period: May and June. Habitat: Venezuela. Warm house.

PLATE 39

**Stanhopea
graveolens** Lᴅʟ.
(= strongly
scented)

Tнᴇ flowers are ivory white or straw-yellow, strongly scented, and are in clusters of three to five; sepals and petals about 6 cm long, turning backwards. The lip is pouched in front, the hypochil orange yellow at the base, the mesochil with fairly long horns and the epichil rhomboidal-crescent shaped with pointed tip. The yellowish-green column has broad wings.

Flowering period: July and August. Habitat: Brazil and Peru.

Cultivation: Owing to the pendent flowers, Stanhopes should be grown on cork or in wooden baskets in the usual compost for epiphytes. Temperate house.

Group 30:
Laeliinae

PLATE 40

**Sophronitis
coccinea** Rchb. f.
(syn. *S. grandiflora*
Ldl.)
(coccinea = scarlet)

Sophronitis cernua
Ldl.
(cernua = arched
over, nodding)

Right (Under) S. cernua

THIS species is the more unassuming of the two illustrated and also the smaller but very attractive on account of its brilliant colour. The pseudo-bulbs, almost cylindrical spindle-shaped, are about 2 cm high along the zig-zag rhizome, the solitary leaves being lateral to it. The leaves are broadly oval, blunt, very fleshy and of a leathery texture, 2.5-3 cm long. The inflorescence is very short and bears one flower as a rule but occasionally as many as four.

The dainty flowers are on thin stalks, bright cinnabar red and about 3 cm across. The pointed sepals and petals are elliptical, the petals rather broader than the sepals. The labellum is broadly ovate, pointed, rather shorter than the petals and clasps the column; it also is cinnabar red with orange-yellow at the base. Warm house.

Flowering period: November to January. Habitat: Brazil.

Left (Above) S. coccinea

THIS species is the most beautiful of all with its comparatively large flowers and shining red colour.

The short, spindle-shaped pseudo-bulbs are 2-3.5 cm high; the leaf is oblong or more tongue-shaped, thick, leathery, short-stalked and about 8 cm long. The flowers are solitary on short peduncles, 5-8 cm across and a brilliant scarlet. The sepals are narrow, oblong, bluntish at the tip and

continued page 161

136

Group 48:
Lycastinae

PLATE 41

Anguloa brevilabris
ROLFE
(= short-lipped)

THE pseudo-bulbs are large, thick, ovate and dark green, 10 to 15 cm
high with four large, oval, plicate leaves up to 50 cm long. The sepals
are golden yellow on both sides, the inner side thickly dotted with
brownish red, as are the shorter petals and the lip also in which the dots
coalesce forming patches. The mobile lip is characteristic of all the species
and swings two and fro with every movement of the plant.

Flowering period: June. Habitat: Colombia.

Anguloas need a complete rest after flowering, during which the leaves
are discarded; they should be kept in a temperate house. After repotting
and during the growing period they need warm house treatment.

PLATE 42

Lycaste aromatica
LDL.
(aromatic = spicey,
from the cinnamon-
like scent of the
flower)

THE pseudo-bulbs are oblong-ovate, up to 6 cm high with one to two leaves, oblong-elliptic in shape, up to 25 cm long and plicate. When the dry leaves are shed, two sharp spines are left on the abscission scar of the pseudo-bulb. The flower stems, usually several together, carry one flower each and are 15 cm high. The erect, strongly scented flowers are about 5 cm across, the sepals oblong, blunt, greenish-orange; the petals elliptic, blunt, orange-yellow and rather shorter. The labellum is three-lobed, very concave at the base; the lateral lobes are oblong and erect, the obovate, longer, central lobe is orange-yellow dotted with red and bears a wide, slightly grooved callus.

Flowering period: April and May. Habitat: Mexico. Temperate house.

PLATE 43

Lycaste skinneri
LDL.
(Named after the
discoverer,
G. Ure-Skinner)

THIS species is of all the Lycastes the most beautiful and rewarding. Not only is it good as a cut flower but also, a good plant for amateurs.

The pseudo-bulbs are oblong-ovate, laterally compressed, up to 8 cm high and bearing two or three leaves which are long-stalked, oblong-elliptic, up to 55 cm long, grooved along the veins and arching over. The lovely flowers are 15 cm across and, like all the Lycastes, solitary on jointed stems about 25-30 cm long. The bracts are fairly small and clasp the stem. The three sepals spread out in a triangular shape and give the flower its characteristic appearance; they are 7 cm long and either pure white or shades of rose pink. The pure white variety is very rare and therefore valuable. The two petals are half as long as the sepals, roundish-oval in shape; they are always erect and very close round the column and are usually rose pink. The labellum is three-lobed, dark purple at the base with yellowish-white, with red dots on the central lobe. The white, red-dotted and hairy column is almost as long as the petals.

Flowering period: October to December. Habitat: Mexico and Guatemala.

This plant wants moderate heat and can therefore be accommodated in a room in winter. The compost is that used for epiphytes with the addition of osmunda, polypodium fibre and sphagnum.

Like all the Lycastes, *L. skinneri* loses its leaves during the resting period and should then be kept completely dry. Temperate house.

PLATE 44

**Zygopetalum
mackayi** Hook.

THIS is the most beautiful and striking of all the species. The large, ovate, pale green pseudo-bulbs, up to 8 cm high, carry many leaves in two ranks; the leaves are oblong lanceolate, about 20 cm long. The peduncle may be up to 50 cm high and bears 5-8 flowers, about 5 cm across and pleasantly scented. The sepals and petals are yellowish green with large red-brown flecks. The labellum is not hairy, crenate in front with a broad white lip disc which is beautifully decorated with violet-blue veins.

Flowering period: November to February. Habitat: Brazil. Warm house.

The usual compost for epiphytes is needed with dried cow dung or horn meal added. In summer the plants need plenty of water.

Group 51:
Maxillarinae

PLATE 45

Maxillaria picta
Hook.
(picta = painted)

This is not a striking, large-flowered orchid but very attractive for the amateur. The pseudo-bulbs are ovate and bear two leaves which are oblong strap-shaped and blunt, up to 25 cm long. The fairly large flowers are solitary on stems 12 cm high, about half the height of the leaves. The colour is pale or whitish yellow with purple cross-stripes. The sepals and petals are tongue-shaped and bluntish; the labellum is three-lobed with blunt side lobes and an oblong frontal lobe.

Flowering period: January to April. Habitat: Brazil and Guayana. Temperate house.

PLATE 46

**Maxillaria
sanderiana**
Rchb. f.
(After Sander, the
famous English
orchid grower)

This is one of the most beautiful and largest-flowered species in the genus but is only valued by amateurs since the flowers are too short-stalked for cutting.

The pseudo-bulbs are almost spherical, about 5 cm high and with two leaves each. The leaves are stalked, lanceolate, pointed, about 30 cm long and 6 cm wide. The peduncle hangs over and bears only one flower.

The large flowers are up to 15 cm across; the ground colour is white. The sepals and petals are elliptical and pointed, the sepals about 6 cm long, the petals shorter. Both are decorated with violet purple flecks which coalesce at the base. The blunt, oval labellum is yellowish patterned with red inside and dark purple outside; it is shorter than the petals and has a prettily waved edge. The column is white with red stripes in front.

Flowering period: August to October. Habitat: Peru at a height of 1500 m and is epiphytic like all the species; it is therefore suitable for indoor cultivation and requires the usual compost for epiphytes. Temperate house.

PLATE 47

Trichopilia tortilis
LDL.
(tortilis = twisted)

THE name refers to the sepals and petals which are always twisted and very characteristic of the species. The pseudo-bulbs are very narrow, 4-8 cm high and 1-1.5 cm thick. The leaf is oblong-elliptic, attenuated to the tip, 10-15 cm long, 3-4 cm wide and grey-green. The inflorescence, which arises laterally from the pseudo-bulb, is pendent and carries one or two flowers. The individual flower is very large, up to 10 cm across, the sepals and petals narrowly lanceolate, spirally twisted, up to 6 cm long, brown with a greenish-yellow edge. The white labellum, trumpet-shaped and about 5.5 cm long, is almost circular in front and deeply cut into two at the frontal end; inside it is fairly closely stippled with pale brownish-red.

Flowering period: December to February. Habitat: Mexico and Guatemala.

Cultivation: the usual compost for epiphytes is required and the plants should have a very light position. Temperate house.

PLATE 48

**Miltonia
spectabilis** LDL.
(= handsome)

THE oval, compressed pseudo-bulbs, up to 7 cm high and bearing two leaves each, arise at short intervals along the creeping rhizome. The leaves are narrow, tongue-shaped, up to 15 cm long. The flower is large and flat, generally solitary on a short stalk, not over-topping the leaves. The white sepals and petals are about 4.5 cm long, narrow, blunt-tipped and spreading. The labellum is broad and oval from a narrow base, with a short recurved tip; the ground colour is white with reddish-violet longitudinal veins, darker in the centre with yellow lamellae at the base. The column is white with two large dark violet auricles.

Flowering period: August. Habitat: Brazil. Warm house.

Group 65:
Sarcanthinae

PLATE 59

Euanthe
sanderiana
SCHLTR.
(syn. *Esmeralda*
sanderiana RCHB.
f.; *Vanda sande-*
riana RCHB. f.)
(Named after
Sander, a well-
known English
grower.)

THIS is the only species in the genus and, in habit, much resembles the two genera *Esmeralda* and *Vanda*, but because of its distinct floral characters, stands mid-way between them.

The monopodial stem reaches a height of 60 cm and the leaves are close and in two ranks. The strap-shaped leaves are up to 45 cm long and 4 cm wide, truncate at the tip with three teeth. The erect, many-flowered inflorescence carries 5-10 very beautiful, loosely arranged flowers and is some 30 cm long. Flowers 9-10 cm across. The sepals and petals are broadly oval, blunt and flat, the lateral ones about 6 cm long, striped and checkered in red-brown on a yellow ground; the central sepal is 5.5 cm long and pale violet blue. The labellum is only 3 cm long, its hypochil semi-globose, yellow with rounded, concave lobes on both sides; the epichil is almost kidney-shaped, blunt with three blunt keels.

Flowering period: October and November. Habitat: Philippines and South East Mindano, epiphytic on trees along the shore. Warm house.

155

PLATE 60

**Phalaenopsis
aphrodite** RCHB. f.

REICHENBACH named this species after Aphrodite, the goddess of love, thereby expressing the idea that, owing to its lovely flowers, this species should be deified. What is so striking is the compactness of the flower due to the way the sepals and petals overlap each other. *P. aphrodite* is very similar to *P. amabilis* which is larger in all its parts.

The stem is short but may carry as many as 8 leaves arranged in two ranks; these are oblong, obovate, fleshy and obliquely crenate at the tip. The large flowers, 8 cm across, 6-15 in number, are arranged alternately along the elegant, arching inflorescence and are pure white. The sepals and petals are very differently shaped; whilst the sepals are oblong-elliptic, the petals are more broadly rhomboidal. The labellum is somewhat shorter than the petals and three-lobed. The sharply jointed, lateral lobes are oval and curved outwards, striped and dotted with red at the base. The three-cornered frontal lobe ends in two prettily curved, thread-like processes.

Flowering period: December to April. Habitat: Philippines. Warm house.